MORE THAN A GAME

RACE, GENDER, AND POLITICS IN SPORTS

MATT DOEDEN

MILLBROOK PRESS · MINNEAPOLIS

Front cover top: Billie Jean King at the Wimbledon Championships in London around 1970.

Front cover bottom: Eric Reid (*left*) and Colin Kaepernick (*right*) kneeling during the anthem at Bank of America Stadium in Charlotte, North Carolina, on September 18, 2016.

Jacket flap: Jackie Robinson (*right*) with Brooklyn Dodgers teammates in 1947.

Back cover: Ibtihaj Muhammed in her fencing gear for the 2016 Olympic Games.

Grateful acknowledgment to Lori Latrice Martin, professor of sociology and African and African American studies at Louisiana State University, and to sensitivity reader Sohum, for providing input on the text.

Millbrook Press
An imprint of Lerner Publishing Group, Inc.
241 First Avenue North
Minneapolis, MN 55401 USA

For reading levels and more information, look up this title at www.lernerbooks.com.

Main body text set in Neo Sans Regular
Typeface provided by Monotype

Library of Congress Cataloging-in-Publication Data

Names: Doeden, Matt, author.
Title: More than a game : race, gender, and politics in sports / Matt Doeden.
Description: Minneapolis : Millbrook Press, [2020] | Includes bibliographical references and index. | Audience: Age 10–18. | Audience: Grade 7–8.
Identifiers: LCCN 2018047656 (print) | LCCN 2019001836 (ebook) | ISBN 9781541562622 (eb pdf) | ISBN 9781541540941 (lb : alk. paper)
Subjects: LCSH: Racism in sports—United States—Juvenile literature. | Sex discrimination in sports—United States—Juvenile literature. | Sports and state— United States—Juvenile literature.
Classification: LCC GV706.32 (ebook) | LCC GV706.32 .D86 2020 (print) | DDC 306.4/83—dc23

LC record available at https://lccn.loc.gov/2018047656

Manufactured in the United States of America
1-45275-38790-2/19/2019

CONTENTS

Colin Kaepernick talks to fans after a game in San Diego, California, on September 1, 2016.

INTRODUCTION

TAKING A KNEE

In the National Football League (NFL), few games mean less than preseason contests. The games don't count in the season's standings. With the regular season about to start, NFL coaches usually leave their starters on the bench to keep them healthy. In a league where almost everything—from the draft to training camp—is filled with hype, preseason games are little more than afterthoughts. So it's pretty hard for one of the games to make national headlines.

Yet in 2016, that's exactly what happened. In Levi's Stadium in Santa Clara, California, the Green Bay Packers defeated the San Francisco 49ers in a preseason game on August 26. Fans would have forgotten the game as soon as it was over, if not for 49ers quarterback Colin Kaepernick.

Before the game even started, Kaepernick made a gesture that would change his career and restart a national debate in the United States. As players and fans stood for the national anthem, a photographer snapped an image of the 49ers bench. There sat Kaepernick, alone in his red number-seven jersey.

The anthem ended. The players took the field, and the game played itself out in front of a crowd of only mildly interested fans. No one mentioned Kaepernick outside of his play during the game. It was a few days later, as the photo of Kaepernick sitting on the bench during the anthem began to spread on Twitter, that his actions drew attention.

Reporters began to ask the quarterback why he hadn't stood with his teammates. "I'm going to continue to stand with the people that are being oppressed," Kaepernick answered. He was referring to African Americans and other people of color in the United States who he believed were the targets of violence and racism by police officers. "This is something that has to change. When there's significant change and I feel that flag represents what it's supposed to represent, and this country is representing people the way that it's supposed to, I'll stand [for the national anthem]."

Kaepernick's words set off a debate. Racial tensions had always existed in the United States. But these tensions had increased in recent years, especially between people of color and police officers. Many people believed that racial profiling and violence against minorities by police were growing worse. They wanted to see this change. Three years earlier, the Black Lives Matter movement had begun in response to the deaths of several African Americans as a result of police actions. The movement campaigns against violence and systemic racism toward black people, often by holding events and protests. Kaepernick's protest supported the movement.

By some accounts, Kaepernick's protest—which he altered the following week by taking a knee instead of remaining seated—was heroic. By others, it was unpatriotic and disrespectful of the men and women of the US Armed Forces and police. Many believe that the US flag represents freedom, sacrifice, and all that is good about the United States. To them, Kaepernick's refusal to stand for the flag and the anthem was a direct insult to those who fought to protect that freedom. And so a small gesture made before the start of a preseason football game became the centerpiece of a national debate. It would change the way many think about racism in the United States, as well as about the responsibilities of star athletes to talk publicly about social issues.

Kaepernick's action was a highly visible collision of sports and culture. The protest changed the way many athletes approached social issues, inspiring them to speak out and talk publicly about problems in society. Kaepernick's movement spread, first to teammates, then to other football players and players in other sports. As more players knelt during the national anthem, many NFL fans became angry about the protests. Some of those fans began boycotting games and products sponsored by the

Colin Kaepernick (*right*) and Eric Reid (*left*) kneel during the national anthem before the game at Levi's Stadium in Santa Clara, California, on September 12, 2016.

league. The boycotts cost the NFL money and enraged many team owners. The protests even drew the attention of US president Donald Trump, who suggested that any player taking a knee should be fired. Suddenly, the national anthem had changed from a pregame formality to a headline-maker.

While Kaepernick had succeeded in shining a spotlight on issues such as racial profiling and police violence, he did so at great cost to himself. Within a year, the former Super Bowl quarterback had been effectively cast out of the NFL. He was unable to secure so much as a backup job with an NFL team.

Kaepernick was out of football, but he was not out of the spotlight. In September 2018, the shoe and clothing company Nike made him one of the centerpieces of its 30th anniversary "Just Do It" campaign. The multi-million-dollar advertising deal for an athlete who didn't even have a job in his sport demonstrated that Kaepernick remained one of the world's most influential athletes. He was the latest proof that sports is about much more than what happens on the playing field. Read on to learn about some of history's key athletes and moments as sports intersected with race, gender, and politics.

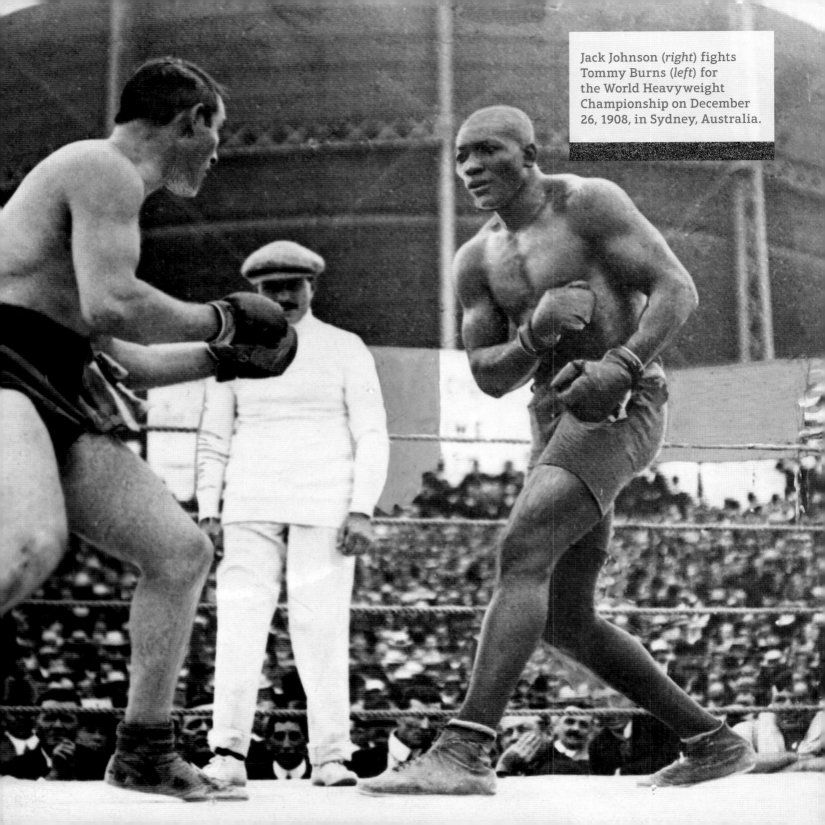

Jack Johnson (*right*) fights Tommy Burns (*left*) for the World Heavyweight Championship on December 26, 1908, in Sydney, Australia.

CHAPTER 1

FROM THE GREAT WHITE HOPE TO BLACK LIVES MATTER

SPORTS AND RACE

Sports have always reflected the beliefs and values of the culture they are part of. Ancient Rome was a harsh, rigid society in which the lowest-ranked people were slaves, many of whom had been enemies captured in battle. Some of those slaves became competitors in Roman gladiator contests and were forced to fight to the death as a form of entertainment for higher-ranked Romans. The early Mayan people played a ball game to please their gods. The gods had an active day-to-day role in Mayan culture, and the game was a serious affair. Winners were celebrated as heroes. Losers could be punished with death.

Modern sports avoid life-and-death stakes. Yet they are still a mirror of our culture. That's especially true with issues of race and equality. Colin Kaepernick's 2016 protest brought the Black Lives Matter movement into football stadiums. Half a century after the US civil rights movement, Kaepernick and the athletes who joined him raised awareness of police violence against people of color. But sports have always reflected the same tensions that shape the societies around them.

The Great White Hope

Boxing was perhaps the most beloved sport in the United States and the world at the beginning of the twentieth century. At the time, the United States was a largely segregated nation. Slavery had been outlawed for less than half a century. The law in many states called for separate services such as schools and public bathrooms for white people and black people. It was a nation divided, and that divide extended to boxing. The big money in boxing was at the heavyweight level, but the top white heavyweight fighters wouldn't accept matches against black boxers. One young black boxer, Jack Johnson, set out to change that. He was ready to grab his piece of the pie. For many, the idea that a black man could face off with a white man in the ring—much less win the heavyweight title—was outrageous. It challenged the common notion in the United States at the time that white men were superior to black men.

Johnson, a hard-hitting slugger nicknamed the Galveston Giant, was among the top black boxers of his era. By 1906, he was ready to fight against a white man for the biggest title in boxing. For two years, Johnson followed world heavyweight champion Tommy Burns around the world. Johnson taunted the white fighter and tried to provoke him into a match.

In 1908, Burns finally gave in to Johnson's challenge. The men met in Sydney, Australia. Over fourteen brutal rounds, Johnson proved beyond any doubt that he was the better boxer. Police finally stopped the fight, fearing that the mostly-white crowd in attendance would riot. Johnson won the match, and his quest to claim the heavyweight title was complete.

To many fans and members of the media, the idea that the world heavyweight champion could be a black man was an insult to white people. Popular writer Jack London called on the world's second-ranked boxer, James Jeffries, to step up and reclaim the title for white boxers. London nicknamed Jeffries the Great White Hope. "Jim Jeffries must now emerge from his alfalfa farm and remove that golden smile from Jack Johnson's face," London wrote. "Jeff, it's up to you. The White Man must be rescued."

That set up one of the most anticipated fights in boxing history. Johnson and Jeffries met on July 4, 1910. People packed the arena in Reno, Nevada, to watch the fight the media called the battle of the century. To some fans, Johnson represented a society that was moving toward equality for all races. To others, a black heavyweight champion was a threat to the idea that whites were the superior race.

The fight itself didn't live up to its billing. Jeffries was past his prime, and Johnson fought circles around the older boxer. When a Johnson punch sent Jeffries to the mat in the fifteenth round, it was all over. Johnson had knocked out the Great White Hope.

More than 16,000 people watched Johnson (*right*) beat Jeffries in Reno.

It was an outrage for many white fans. The result set off a wave of violence against black people across the United States. No one is sure how many died. Estimates say as many as twenty-six people, mostly black Americans, were killed in riots set off by the result of the match. The era of white dominance in boxing was over, even if the end came at a terrible cost.

Jesse Owens and the Black Eagles

Germany in the 1930s was a nation of hatred and racism. As Adolf Hitler and the Nazi Party rose to power, they set forth an agenda of prejudice toward minorities. Nazis advanced the idea that white Germans were part of a superior race. This idea led to the Holocaust, the systematic killing of minorities—especially Jewish people—in Germany and German-held areas.

That made the 1936 Olympic Games in Berlin, Germany, a complicated affair for other participants. The United States and several other nations considered a boycott of the games in protest of the German government's policies of hate. But in the end, US athletes made the trip to Berlin. It was an uneasy journey for minorities on the US team, particularly Jewish athletes. US officials pulled runners Marty Glickman and Sam Stoller from a racing event, seemingly to avoid offending Hitler. The bigotry was hard on the team's black athletes as well. German officials mocked the United States for allowing black athletes to compete, referring to black athletes as non-human.

In the face of intense racism, eighteen black US athletes took home medals from Berlin. None of them did so more famously than runner Jesse Owens. Owens won four gold medals in track-and-field events, all of them under Hitler's sharp and unhappy gaze.

After Owens defeated Germany's Luz Long in the long jump competition, the German was the first to congratulate him. "It took a lot of courage for [Long] to befriend me in front of Hitler," Owens said. "Hitler must have gone crazy watching us embrace."

It was a symbolic victory for minority athletes and a defeat for Hitler's hateful policies. But the eighteen medal-winning athletes, nicknamed the Black Eagles, didn't get a hero's welcome when they returned home to the United States. Instead, they got a stark reminder that while racism and bigotry

Owens's Olympic medals were in the 100-meter race, the 200-meter race, the 4-by-100-meter relay, and the long jump.

was at its peak in Germany, conditions back in the United States also included hostility and inequality. Owens was an American hero to many. Yet he never got so much as a congratulations from President Franklin Delano Roosevelt's White House. At a reception in his honor at a New York City hotel, Owens had to take the service elevator. The normal guest elevator was for white people only.

Jackie Robinson and Baseball's Color Barrier

The first half of the twentieth century was a golden age for baseball. It became the most popular sport in the United States and earned the nickname "the national pastime." White players from this time such as Ty Cobb, Babe Ruth, and Ted Williams are giants in Major League Baseball (MLB) history. But others who were every bit as good are much less famous. Black players such as Cool Papa Bell, Josh Gibson, and Satchel Paige were also among the greats of the era. However, these talented players were left to build their legends in the Negro Leagues, professional baseball leagues for people of color. The Negro Leagues included many teams and leagues around the United States.

MLB team owners barred players of color for more than sixty years. The path to change started in 1941 when the United States entered World War II (1939–1945). Americans of all racial and religious backgrounds—including many of the day's biggest baseball stars—fought side by side in Europe and Asia. Some baseball fans wondered, if men of different races could fight and die together in defense of their country, why couldn't they share a baseball dugout?

The idea that MLB should end its long history of segregation met with strong resistance. The US civil rights movement had yet to pick up steam. Prejudice and racism remained widespread in the United States. Most team owners rejected the idea of allowing black players on big-league teams. Likewise, owners of Negro Leagues teams opposed integration because they didn't want to lose players to MLB.

Yet some baseball officials wanted to put an end to the sport's exclusion of people of color. Among them was Branch Rickey, general manager of the National League's Brooklyn Dodgers. Rickey was a proven winner. He didn't shy away from decisions that might draw criticism. In 1945, he began scouting the Negro Leagues for a player who could break baseball's color barrier and change the sport forever.

Before playing for the Montreal Royals, Jackie Robinson *(second from right)* played professional football in Hawaii and baseball for the Kansas City Monarchs of the Negro American League.

Rickey knew that MLB's first black athlete in the modern era would face attention and anger unlike any player before him. It had to be someone who could handle himself both on and off the baseball diamond. Rickey found what he was looking for in an infielder named Jackie Robinson. Robinson was a sweet-swinging, smooth-fielding speedster well suited to the MLB game. What really set Robinson apart was his cool and calm demeanor. He had a military background and had once refused to sit in the back of a segregated bus while serving in the US Army. "[Robinson] knew how to handle pressure," said teammate Don Newcombe. "He had [racial abuse] happen to him while he was in the military."

Rickey signed Robinson to a contract. In 1946, Robinson joined the Montreal Royals of the International League, a minor-league team of the Dodgers. The twenty-seven-year-old quickly erased any doubts about whether he belonged. Robinson led the league with a .349 batting average and forty stolen bases.

Robinson played for the Dodgers from 1947 to 1956. After retiring from baseball, he became a civil rights activist.

The real test came a year later on April 15, 1947. Robinson took the field as a Brooklyn Dodger and officially ended baseball's six decades of segregation. The reception he got was sadly predictable. He was booed and taunted by white spectators. Hate mail poured in from all across the country. When the team was on the road, he was barred from staying in some hotels with his teammates. He received death threats. Even some of his teammates plotted to get him thrown off the team.

The constant abuse might have broken some players, but Robinson was prepared. He knew the cost of standing up for his rights, and he held his head high through it all. Slowly, many fans began to pay more attention to his play on the field than to what he represented as an agent of change. In spite of all of the distractions, Robinson thrived in the big leagues. He batted .297, stole twenty-nine bases, and won the National League Rookie of the Year award.

Despite the negative responses, Robinson also drew fans to the ballpark by the thousands. Baseball was a business, and Robinson opened new streams of income for MLB teams. Much of that money came from minority fans eager to buy tickets to see the young star in action. The novelty of a black Major Leaguer also brought in white fans, even if some of them were there to boo. When the hiring of Robinson proved to be a financial gain for his team and the league, it didn't take long for other teams to follow the Dodgers' example. In July 1947, the Cleveland Indians made Larry Doby the American League's first black player. The floodgates opened and more black players joined MLB in the following years.

The fall of baseball's color barrier served as a sign of bigger changes in US culture. Over the next two decades, the civil rights movement grew in strength. Black Americans slowly gained rights that had been denied to them for hundreds of years. From the integration of schools and other public buildings to diverse athletes in pro sports, the civil rights movement would eventually end legal segregation entirely. Although we typically think of the civil rights movement as beginning in the 1950s, Jackie Robinson, like Jack Johnson and Jesse Owens, is among a group of pioneers who fought for racial justice even before the movement was in full swing.

BAYLOR SITS OUT

The road to integration in professional sports leagues was not easy. Even after black athletes were allowed to play, white people inside and outside of the leagues didn't always welcome them. Black athletes faced racism from fans, other teams, and even teammates. They traveled to cities that were hostile to the idea of equal rights. Even a black athlete sleeping in the same hotel as white teammates was a problem at times.

Such was the case for National Basketball Association (NBA) legend Elgin Baylor. In 1959, the rookie traveled to Charleston, West Virginia, with his Minneapolis Lakers teammates. He did not get a warm welcome. The team hotel was reserved for white people only and Baylor and several black teammates were refused rooms. The entire team joined Baylor in leaving the hotel to find a place in town where they could stay together. Baylor said that he couldn't even find a decent restaurant in town that would serve him. He had to eat cold food from a grocery store instead.

Baylor protested his abuse the only way he knew how. He refused to play in the game. He sat on the bench in street clothes as his Lakers lost to the Cincinnati Royals 95–91.

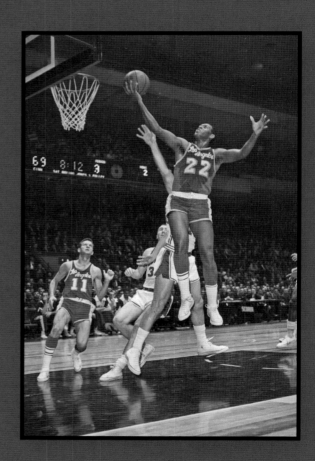

Baylor (*center*) played in eleven All-Star Games during his fourteen-year NBA career.

Texas Western guard Orsten Artis (*left*) and coach Don Haskins leave the court after their semifinal game in the 1966 NCAA basketball tournament. Texas Western beat Utah 85–78.

Texas Western Changes the Game

The 1960s were a time of radical change in American culture and in sports. The US Civil Rights Act of 1964 barred racial segregation in schools. Black athletes, long denied the chance to play in certain leagues, were walking through doors that had finally opened to them. Among them was the right to compete in major college sports.

At the time, college basketball was rapidly becoming more popular. The University of Kentucky had one of the nation's top basketball programs and an all-white team. In 1966, the Kentucky Wildcats advanced to the title game in the National Collegiate Athletic Association Men's Basketball Tournament. That was of little surprise to anyone. However, their opponent shook up the college basketball landscape. The Texas Western Miners, led by coach Don Haskins, featured a starting lineup entirely of black players. It was something that no major college team had ever done before. Some basketball fans believed that black players lacked the ability to succeed without white players to lead them. Yet the Miners had lost just one game all season, shattering that belief.

The title game represented a clash between a segregated past and a future that judged players on their skill rather than the color of their skin. Ten players stepped onto the court for the opening tip-off. All five Kentucky players were white. All five Texas Western players were black.

Leading up to the game, many reporters suggested that the Miners would have no chance. They said Texas Western's style lacked the control needed to beat a team as good as Kentucky. Kentucky head coach Adolph Rupp vowed before the game that five black players would never beat his Wildcats.

Texas Western upset its critics. The Miners were calm and in control on the court, carefully breaking down the Wildcats on their way to a 72–65 victory. "We played the most intelligent, the most boring, the most disciplined game of them all," said Miners guard Willie Worsley.

The Civil Rights Act had formally banned segregation in college sports, and Texas Western's championship struck down the idea that black players couldn't win without white players. One more barrier to equality had been demolished.

Raising a Fist

Thirty-two years after racial tensions affected the 1936 Olympic Games in Germany, another Olympic moment sent a message about social justice. US athletes traveled to Mexico City, Mexico, for the 1968 Olympic Games. Racism was still widespread in the United States at the time. Many felt that despite victories such as the Civil Rights Act, the fight for social justice needed to continue.

US sprinters Tommie Smith and John Carlos were ready to take a stand at the Olympics. On the morning of October 16, they took part in the men's 200-meter finals. Smith blazed out of the starting

BREAKING BARRIERS

Jackie Robinson is the most famous athlete to break a racial barrier in sports. Yet baseball wasn't the only sport that banned people of color. Many sports figures changed sports, and society, by breaking down racial barriers.

Willie O'Ree

In 1958, Willie O'Ree joined the Boston Bruins and became the first black player in the National Hockey League. O'Ree didn't just overcome a racial barrier to succeed in hockey. He also overcame a physical barrier. He was mostly blind in one eye after being struck in the face with a puck.

Bill Russell

Bill Russell became an NBA legend as a center for the Boston Celtics. He also made a major impact as a head coach. In 1966, Russell became the NBA's first black head coach. He led the Celtics to championships in 1968 and 1969.

Charlie Sifford

Charlie Sifford began a quest to join the Professional Golf Association tour in 1952. The black player endured threats and racial taunts. Sifford finally broke golf's color barrier in 1961. He won twenty-two events and paved the way for minority athletes to break into the game.

Wayne Embry

After eleven years as a professional basketball player, Wayne Embry became general manager of the NBA's Milwaukee Bucks in 1972. He took control of the team's roster and overall operation. Embry was the first black general manager in major pro sports.

Wendell Oliver Scott

On December 1, 1963, Wendell Oliver Scott took the checkered flag to win a race at Speedway Park in Jacksonville, Florida. Scott was the first black driver ever to win at NASCAR's highest level.

Tony Dungy

When the Indianapolis Colts beat the Chicago Bears in the 2007 Super Bowl, head coach Tony Dungy made history. He became the first black head coach to win a Super Bowl. The opposing coach, Lovie Smith, became the first black head coach to lose a Super Bowl.

Carlos (*right*) had left his black gloves at the hotel. So, Smith (*center*) gave him one of his to wear for their salute.

blocks. He pulled away from the other racers and crossed the finish line with a world-record time of 19.83 seconds. As the crowd roared, Carlos finished third. He was just a fraction of a second behind Australia's Peter Norman.

Smith and Carlos made their way to the ceremony to receive their medals. They took off their shoes as a way to protest poverty. They wore beads and scarves to protest lynching—the violent killing of people, especially black men, by hanging in the United States. As the "Star-Spangled Banner" played, the two men quietly bowed their heads. Each raised a single gloved fist into the air to salute the black power movement. The movement had grown as a contrast to the nonviolent civil rights movement. The black power movement encouraged black people to take pride in African American culture, control their own images, and determine their own destinies.

"I looked at my feet in my high socks and thought about all the black poverty I'd seen from Harlem to East Texas," Carlos later wrote. "I fingered my beads and thought about the pictures I'd seen of [lynchings in] the South. . . . I felt that my country was traveling at a snail's pace toward something that should be obvious to all people of good will. Then the anthem started and we raised our fists into the air."

Their gestures sent shock waves through the stadium. "As the anthem began and the crowd saw us raise our fists, the stadium became eerily quiet," Carlos wrote. "There's something awful about hearing fifty thousand people go silent, like being in the eye of a hurricane." The silence was quickly replaced by a shower of boos.

The moment perfectly captured the divided racial climate of the day. Smith and Carlos had succeeded in spreading their message, but it came at a cost. Olympic officials quickly expelled the athletes from the arena and stripped them of their medals. They were banned from further competitions. Instead of returning home as Olympic heroes, they were widely criticized in the United States. Carlos and Smith both received death threats.

Yet Smith said he did not regret his actions. He knew that standing to receive his medal at the Olympics would be his best chance to spread his message to a huge audience. "We had to be seen," he said, "because we couldn't be heard."

Arthur Ashe Breaks Through

In the 1970s, not many sports had fewer people of color than tennis. Black players faced overt racism. Additionally, many neighborhoods where young black athletes lived simply didn't have tennis courts that would allow them to master the game. And some places that gave young players a chance to improve, such as private tennis clubs, prevented black athletes from playing. Yet that didn't stop Arthur Ashe from trying to become the sport's first black superstar.

It wasn't easy. Ashe grew up in Richmond, Virginia, during a time when segregation was alive and well. He was barred from using his school's courts to play against white opponents. As a high school senior, he moved to St. Louis, Missouri, where he had more opportunity to compete.

Arthur Ashe remains the only African American man to win the singles title at Wimbledon.

Despite the hurdles he faced, Ashe blazed a trail. In 1962, he became the first African American National Junior Indoor champion. That fall, he accepted a tennis scholarship to the University of California, Los Angeles. Once he turned professional in 1969, his world-class talent was obvious. So was his leadership. Ashe became the president of the Association of Tennis Professionals in 1974.

The highlight of his career came in the 1975 Wimbledon tennis tournament in London, England. Ashe faced the heavily favored Jimmy Connors, a fellow American, in the final match. The pair had clashed before, and Connors had won all of their previous matches. But this time, Ashe was on his game. He smashed one big shot after another at Connors to win in four sets. Ashe became the first black man to win Wimbledon and helped pave the way for future African American stars such as Venus and Serena Williams.

The Redskins Debate

Fans of the NFL's Washington Redskins often wear their team colors with pride at their home stadium in Washington, DC, and on the road. But as Washington fans made their way to a 2014 game against the Minnesota Vikings in Minneapolis, Minnesota, many of them hid their caps and covered their jerseys. That's because hundreds of American Indians and their supporters were marching outside of the stadium in protest of Washington's team nickname and logo. The logo is a warrior with exaggerated features that the protestors viewed as mocking American Indian appearance and identity.

Many pro and college sports have used team nicknames based on American Indians. Supporters claim that this honors American Indians, but others, including many American Indians, see it differently. They feel the nicknames and logos put down American Indians and ignore the damage to American Indian cultures caused by European colonization of North America. For some, any nickname based on American Indians is offensive. Yet one stood out as the most racist for its focus on skin color: the Redskins.

The protest in Minneapolis was peaceful. Yet the protesters were not shy about shouting their opinions at anyone who walked by wearing Washington gear. Many Washington fans, uneasy about the protest, chose to cover their colors rather than face the shouts.

Organizers estimated that 5,000 people participated in the protest of the Redskins in Minneapolis.

The protest came at a time when the debate over American Indian team nicknames had reached new heights. From high schools to colleges to the professional ranks, many teams were giving up the nicknames and images of American Indians. Among them was the University of North Dakota, long known as the Fighting Sioux. In 2015, officials who oversaw college sports increased pressure on the university to take on a new nickname. They became the Fighting Hawks. Three years later, baseball's Cleveland Indians agreed to remove their team logo from uniforms. The Chief Wahoo logo was a smiling, cartoonish American Indian.

Yet the NFL and the Redskins refused to change either the nickname or logo. In 2018, NFL commissioner Roger Goodell pointed to a survey that showed most American Indians were not offended by the team. "This issue has been around for several decades if not longer," Goodell said. "A . . . poll that came out in [2016] . . . said nine out of ten Native Americans do not take that in a negative fashion—the Redskins' logo or the Redskins' name, and they support it."

The debate over Washington's nickname rages on. Some media outlets refuse to use the nickname. People have boycotted the team and the NFL. Some American Indians have made heartfelt pleas to Redskins ownership, asking them to have the nickname changed. Despite all the controversy, it appears unlikely the nickname and logo are going anywhere anytime soon.

Ibtihaj Muhammad Stands Tall

The sport of fencing doesn't often make national headlines in the United States. But that's what happened during the 2016 Olympic Games in Rio de Janeiro, Brazil. US fencer Ibtihaj Muhammad stepped out to compete in her event, the saber. Muhammad was dressed in her white fencing uniform. Her head was wrapped in a hijab, a traditional covering for the hair and neck of Muslim women. She was the first American ever to wear one in Olympic competition.

Muhammad's Olympic appearance came at a time when Donald Trump was running to become US president. Trump was arguing for a reduction in immigration from countries that had mostly Muslim people. He suggested these immigrants could be extremists who would commit terrorist attacks. The

Muhammad's memoir, *Proud: My Fight for an Unlikely American Dream*, was published in 2018.

fencing event was a chance for Muhammad to show the world that wearing a hijab was something a strong, independent woman could do while representing the United States.

Muhammad did not earn a medal competing alone, but she was part of the four-member US fencing team that took home a bronze medal. As she stood for the medal ceremony still wearing her hijab, she became the first American Muslim woman to earn a medal for her country. She proudly received her medal while honoring her religion and culture.

Muhammad embraced the opportunity to be a role model as both a Muslim woman and an American. "I believe . . . we are in a really [strange] time in our country, where people are comfortable saying things about particular groups, and they encourage fear, and they encourage violence, and I want to challenge those ideas," she said. "I feel I have to use my platform as an athlete to speak up, and hopefully provide change in this country."

The Kaepernick Effect

In 2014, some NBA players wore T-shirts before games with messages protesting police violence against people of color. Such protests weren't uncommon at the top levels of sports. Colin Kaepernick's 2016 protest for social justice during the national anthem inspired even more athletes to take action. In the months that followed, other players from the NFL, along with athletes from different sports, protested in their own ways. Some teams held hands or locked arms during the anthem as a show of unity with one another and with people experiencing racism. Many Women's National Basketball Association (WNBA) players wore shirts with messages such as "Black Lives Matter." Athletes from a wide range of sports took to social media to call for social change. Meanwhile, other athletes spoke out against such protests. They pledged their support to police officers and praised them for the difficult jobs they do.

Meanwhile, the man who helped start it all remained without a job. Kaepernick's involvement with the movement had taken root at the cost of his career. Even though he wasn't making news on the field, he had become one of the most talked about people in the nation. "Kaepernick is more than

A POWERFUL PROTEST

Another protest on a basketball court in 2014 grabbed national attention. This one didn't come from star players in a pro league. But the protest itself was so packed with emotion that it was almost impossible to ignore.

Ariyana Smith and the Knox College women's basketball team were set to play Fontbonne University in St. Louis, Missouri. At the time, headlines were filled with protests over police violence in Ferguson, Missouri. Officials there had just decided that police officer Darren Wilson would not be charged with a crime for his deadly shooting of Michael Brown. Like many others, Smith was troubled by the shooting as well as by the violence against protesters that followed. As the national anthem started, she left the team's bench and stood under one of the baskets.

Smith raised her hands in the air. Then she crumpled to the floor, as if shot. She lay there perfectly still for four minutes and thirty seconds. The time stood for the four hours and thirty minutes that Michael Brown lay dead in the street. "I knew it was going to shock people," Smith said. "I knew they were going to be upset, but I couldn't let that stop me."

just an athlete these days," wrote Kent Babb of the *Washington Post*. To some, Kaepernick was a rich, spoiled athlete who didn't value his own good fortune or the vital work of police officers. To others, he had become a powerful voice for social justice and a symbol of the power star athletes could use to bring about change.

Players from nearly every NFL team participated in Kaepernick's protest in some way. Members of the Indianapolis Colts knelt with linked arms during the national anthem on September 24, 2017.

Women's professional baseball players kneel with a coach in the 1940s. The league's story was featured in the 1992 movie *A League of Their Own*.

CHAPTER 2

EQUAL RIGHTS, EQUAL OPPORTUNITIES

GENDER AND SEXUALITY IN SPORTS

In much the same way that sports has held up a mirror to racial divides, it has also reflected changing views on gender and sexual identity. Men dominated sports well into the 1900s. Some people thought women were too delicate for the rough-and-tumble world of sports. Pierre de Coubertin, known as the father of the modern Olympics, was one of them. In 1896, he said, "No matter how toughened a sportswoman may be, her organism is not cut out to sustain certain shocks."

De Coubertin's words spoke to a common feeling of the time. Echoes of the idea would persist for another century. But just as the twentieth century saw people of color gain equal rights on and off the field of play, it saw opportunity grow for others too. From the moment tennis player Charlotte Cooper of the United Kingdom won the first ever women's Olympic gold medal in 1900, the march toward gender equality in sports was on.

It took a war to give women their first taste of professional team sports. When the United States entered World War II in 1941, young men around the nation flocked to the military to defend their country. Women served in non-combat jobs and filled domestic roles that men had occupied. That often meant working on farms or in factories. But for a select few, it was a chance to fill a void in the sports world.

The All-American Girls Professional Baseball League (AAGPBL) formed in 1943. The league existed for eleven seasons. It peaked in popularity around 1948 when it featured ten teams. Yet, however open-minded the AAGPBL may have seemed, the league was still very aware of social norms of the day. Only white women were allowed to play. All of the athletes who competed in the league went to a special charm school that emphasized "ladylike" manners. Their uniforms were belted, above-the-knee dresses. The league gave every player a beauty kit in an effort to make the players as physically attractive as possible. Athletes were barred from smoking or drinking alcohol in public. They weren't even allowed to have short hair.

The AAGPBL's obvious sexism would not have a place in modern sports. But when the league started in 1943, allowing women to play pro baseball was a new idea. And it set the stage for bigger and better things to come.

By the early 1970s, an equal rights movement for women was in full swing in the United States. Encouraged by the successes of the US civil rights movement, women sought equal rights in areas such as public education, personal healthcare, and sports. College sports had become a big business. It raked in money in tickets, jerseys, and TV deals. In return, colleges awarded valuable sports scholarships to athletes—mostly young men. That gave male athletes educational opportunities they might not have had without sports. Equal rights activists said it was time for women to get those same opportunities.

In 1972, the US government passed a law called Title IX. It stated that no person could be denied education benefits based on gender. As simple as Title IX sounds, it had major effects on women's college sports. Suddenly, schools receiving federal money had to offer equal opportunities to women and men. That meant they had to add women's sports programs at roughly the same rate as men's sports. Colleges also had to offer athletic scholarships to women. The law opened the way for a wave of new sports and education opportunities for women. Women's college athletics have grown more popular ever since.

The Battle of the Sexes

Women's sports at the professional level did not yet have widespread acceptance in the early 1970s. However, one sport where women had begun to gain a foothold was tennis. Players such as Australia's Margaret Court proved that women's tennis could be just as exciting as the men's game. She thrilled fans by winning all of the major pro tournaments in 1970. Yet some people still regarded it as a men's sport, including Bobby Riggs. Riggs was a former men's tennis champion. He claimed the women's game was inferior. He said that even at age fifty-five he could beat the best women of any age. Riggs backed up his boast on May 13, 1973, beating thirty-year-old Court in two sets.

Billie Jean King is carried onto the court on a throne for her match against Bobby Riggs.

Court was one of the top women's tennis players of the day. But Riggs really wanted to play against twenty-nine-year-old Billie Jean King, widely seen as the best female tennis player in the world. King declined Riggs' offer at first. But after the ABC television network offered a $100,000 winner-take-all prize, she finally accepted. The match, called the Battle of the Sexes, was on.

On September 20, 1973, more than thirty thousand fans packed the Houston Astrodome in Texas to see the match. Millions more tuned in on TV. It was a wild show. Riggs and King exchanged joke gifts and traded insults before the match. But once the action started, it looked like Riggs would again back up his boasting. He jumped out to a 3-2 lead in the first set. That's when King took over. She was at the peak of her career. She wore down the older Riggs, who grew visibly tired as the match went on.

King won the match, taking all three sets. She threw her racket high into the air in celebration after winning the final point to secure victory. "I thought it would set [the women's rights movement] back fifty years if I didn't win that match," she said. Critics have called the match little more than a moneymaking stunt. But some believe it was an important moment that helped fuel future gains in women's tennis, as well as other sports.

Game Changers: The 1999 US Women's National Team

One of the biggest boosts women's sports has ever received in the United States came from an unlikely source: soccer. It is the world's most popular sport. Yet soccer has never grabbed the same level of popularity in the United States. So when the United States was set to host the 1999 Women's World Cup, some players were concerned about fan interest. "We were worried because we didn't want to play that World Cup before empty stands in big stadiums," said US player Kristine Lilly.

Yet the stadiums were far from empty. The US team had won Olympic gold three years earlier. It was ultra-talented and brimming with well-known players. Fans loved stars such as Lilly, Mia Hamm, and Briana Scurry. US media coverage of the World Cup grew as the team marched toward the final match. By the time the final between the United States and China was set, much of the nation was caught up

The United States' win at the 1999 Women's World Cup is still the only time the host country has won.

in a soccer craze. Television ratings were sky high. People everywhere were talking about the team and the tournament. No US women's team had ever before created that kind of widespread interest.

An estimated 40 million Americans tuned in to watch the final. That was more US fans than had ever watched a women's or men's soccer match. And they were treated to one of the most amazing and memorable games in the history of US sports. For 120 minutes, the two sides locked in an intense and action-packed scoreless tie. That meant the title came down to a penalty shootout. It was the ultimate soccer drama.

In the fifth and final round of penalty kicks, defender Brandi Chastain had a chance to win it for the United States. Chastain had missed a penalty kick against China just three months before. She wasted little time shooting the ball. She swung her left foot, swiftly booting the ball toward the right corner of China's goal. Goalkeeper Gao Hong dove and stretched. But the ball whizzed past her fingers. Goal! The stadium erupted as fans celebrated the home team's win. Chastain ripped off her white jersey and dropped to her knees as her teammates sprinted across the field to celebrate with her.

It was an incredible moment in sports. The US women's team had captured the entire nation's imagination in a way that few had before. And it showed that the United States was ready to embrace a women's team every bit as much as a men's team.

Michael Sam's Quest

Progress for gay athletes in sports lagged behind gender equality. By the 2000s, openly gay players in individual sports and women's team sports were common. Gay athletes such as soccer's Abby Wambach and the WNBA's Sheryl Swoopes were proud of their sexuality. But progress was far slower in men's team sports. In 2013, NBA center Jason Collins came out as the first openly gay player in a major US men's team sport. Collins was a veteran who had entered the league in 2001. He'd already had a long and successful career, and current and former players responded positively to the news. Collins played briefly for the Brooklyn Nets in 2014, and he retired later that year.

In 2014, Michael Sam was looking to break into the NFL as the league's first openly gay player. He was a star defensive end for the University of Missouri football team. As a college senior, Sam was one of the best players in the United States. He won the Southeastern Conference Defensive Player of the Year award. His college production had been outstanding, but he was small for an NFL defensive end. League scouts projected him as a third- or fourth-round pick in the 2014 NFL Draft.

Michael Sam (*center*) won the Arthur Ashe Courage Award at the 2014 ESPY awards for coming out as gay and challenging stereotypes and bigotry in sports and society.

Players who aren't expected to be chosen in the first round of the draft don't usually draw a lot of attention from fans. Sam would have likely been a footnote in the intense media coverage leading up to the event, if not for one thing. In February, just a few months before the draft, he publicly came out as gay. That was earth-shattering news in the ultra-macho NFL. Several NFL players had come out as gay after their careers were over. But no one had ever played in the league while openly gay.

Sam immediately became the focus of media attention. "I just want to make sure I could tell my story the way I want to tell it," Sam said during an endless stream of interviews about his decision to go public. "I just want to own my truth."

Draft day came. The first and second rounds passed. So did the third and the fourth—the rounds in which NFL scouts had expected a team to select Sam. He watched as rounds five and six went by. Still his name was not called. Finally, in the seventh round, the St. Louis Rams made Sam the 249th overall draft pick. Cameras filmed him as he celebrated by kissing his boyfriend.

"When I was drafted I thought the headline would be 'NFL has first openly gay player,' but instead it was 'Sam kisses boyfriend,' " Sam said. "Should I have kissed a girl? The media made it a distraction."

That media distraction was only the beginning. From the moment Sam reported to the Rams, he was hounded by questions from reporters. So were his teammates. Reporters asked if sharing a locker room with a gay player made the players uncomfortable. The ESPN television network even aired a special report detailing Sam's showering habits. The report said that he waited to shower until his teammates had left. The network later apologized for running the story.

In the end, Sam's quest to become the league's first openly gay player fell short. He failed to make the Rams' opening-day team. He was one of many rookies cut by teams after playing in the preseason. He briefly joined the Dallas Cowboys, but he never played in an NFL regular-season game. Sam played in a single Canadian Football League game in 2015 before retiring from the sport.

Fallon Fox: Fighting for Acceptance

It was a fight that sparked a nationwide debate. In September 2014, mixed martial arts (MMA) fighter Fallon Fox beat Tamikka Brents. The fight lasted barely two minutes. Fox overpowered Brents in every way in a fight that sent Brents to the hospital with a brain injury and a broken eye socket.

MMA is no stranger to extreme violence. Broken bones and head injuries are common when trained fighters battle. Yet this fight was different to some MMA fans. Fox was fighting in the women's division. Assigned the gender of boy at birth, Fox had undergone sex confirmation surgery in 2006 to transition her body to more closely match her female gender identity.

Fox's gender status started a lively debate. Many praised her as a pioneer for being the first openly transgender MMA athlete. Others disagreed with her decision to fight in a woman's division.

After retiring from football, Sam became an author and motivational speaker.

Fox training at the Midwest Training Center in suburban Chicago.

They felt that her biological sex at birth provided unfair physical advantages. Fox was stunned by the wave of angry feelings. She said, "The scope of anger and vitriol [nasty criticism] that I received initially . . . That was disheartening, tragic. It was mind-blowing."

Fox's MMA career was brief. She went 5–1 in just six pro fights. But her story opened new lines of debate about what defines gender and the inclusion of transgender athletes in certain sports.

WE GOT NEXT:
DAWN OF THE WNBA

By the 1990s, several professional women's sports leagues had come and gone. None had proven to have staying power. That changed in 1997 when the WNBA tipped off. It built on the growing popularity of women's basketball both at the college level and on international stages such as the Olympics. The league was primed for success. It had the backing of NBA owners and a television contract to bring in money. Teams had star power with players such as Sheryl Swoopes, Lisa Leslie, and Rebecca Lobo.

Over the years, the WNBA's fan base grew as superstars such as Maya Moore and Breanna Stewart emerged to thrill fans. Its popularity has never equaled that of the NBA or other major men's sports leagues. WNBA players don't earn massive multi-million-dollar contracts like male players do. WNBA games receive less media attention. Yet after two decades, the league is still going strong. The WNBA is proof that there is a growing place for professional women's team sports in the United States.

The first WNBA game was between the New York Liberty and the Los Angeles Sparks on June 21, 1997.

Me Too:
Standing Up to Sexual Abuse

The Me Too movement is a campaign to help survivors, particularly women of color, heal and talk publicly about their experiences with sexual harassment and abuse. It was founded in 2006 by Tarana Burke but began trending on social media in 2017. As the movement widened, it inspired a diverse group of people to speak out against sexual predators. It grew rapidly and helped victims tell their stories without shame.

The movement extended from Hollywood to the business world and into sports. Survivors called out some athletes for their abusive actions. Leagues and teams responded by promising to provide players with better education about sexual harassment and abuse. High-profile athletes such as NFL quarterback Jameis Winston were suspended for alleged abuse.

Other athletes came forward with their own stories. Most notable among them was Aly Raisman and other members of the US women's gymnastics team. In 2016, the *Indianapolis Star* newspaper published an explosive report on gymnastics team doctor Larry Nassar. The report said that Nassar had sexually abused children and young women who were supposed to be under his care.

As the Me Too movement gained momentum, more and more gymnasts stepped forward. They added their accusations against Nassar to an ever-growing list. Among them was Olympic medalist McKayla Maroney. "[The abuse] started when I was 13 years old," Maroney wrote in an October 2017 Twitter post. "It didn't end until I left the sport. . . . Our silence has given the wrong people power for too long, and it's time to take our power back. And remember, it's never too late to speak up."

Maroney's story and similar stories told by many fellow gymnasts rocked the sports world. Nassar's actions drove home the importance of the Me Too movement. Nassar was eventually charged, convicted, and imprisoned for his crimes. In 2018, ESPN's ESPY Awards honored the young women who had spoken out against him with the Arthur Ashe Award for Courage. Sarah Klein, who identifies as the first person to be abused by Nassar, said the women on stage at the ESPYs were there "to present an image for the world to see: a portrait of survival, a new vision of courage."

At the 2018 ESPY Awards, survivors of Nassar's abuse accepted the Arthur Ashe Courage Award. At the time, Aly Raisman (*right*) said, "We may suffer alone, but we survive together."

In 1944, major league baseball player Ted Williams (*right*) became a Second Lieutenant in the Marine Corps.

CHAPTER 3

PATRIOTISM AND PROTEST
SPORTS AND WAR

Sports are supposed to be an escape. Fans usually don't want to be distracted by more serious issues when they're rooting for their favorite teams and athletes. Yet sports can never be fully separated from world events, and their connection is never clearer than in times of war. In dark times, people turn to sports to take their minds off their troubles. During wartime, sports also serve as important platforms for both protest and patriotism.

World War II Changes the Face of Sports

World War II had a huge impact around the world, and the changes were reflected in sports. Everyday life was on hold for more than half a decade as fighting raged between the world's biggest powers. The bloody war postponed major international sporting events such as the Olympic Games, soccer World Cups, and the Tour de France bicycle race.

When the United States entered the war in 1941, the nation diverted all of its rubber resources to the effort. As a result, many auto and motorcycle races were cancelled. Meanwhile, young men enlisted by the millions in the US armed forces and went to war. Athletes were no exception. Baseball was the nation's most popular team sport, and some of its biggest stars exchanged their baseball uniforms for military uniforms. Joe DiMaggio, Ted Williams, and Yogi Berra were among many ballplayers who gave up much of the prime of their careers to fight for their country. Not all of the

THE CHRISTMAS DAY TRUCE

World War I (1914–1918) was a brutal and bloody conflict. Some of the worst fighting occurred in the trenches of Europe as soldiers butchered one another by the millions. Opposing soldiers lined up in trenches dug in the ground and attacked one another with guns and bombs. The death toll was massive. Yet in all the darkness of that war, one day stood out as a cause for hope.

On December 25, 1914, German and British troops called an unofficial and unplanned truce. On their own, they put down their weapons and greeted one another with Christmas wishes. The enemies shook hands, exchanged gifts, and sang songs.

According to many reports of the Christmas Day Truce, sports provided enemy soldiers a chance to interact with one another in a way that seemed almost impossible in such a setting. Soccer was the game of choice in both Britain and Germany. Informal matches broke out along the battle lines. Soldiers who had been desperately trying to kill one another took time off from the mayhem of war to play soccer and celebrate together. The fighting resumed the next day.

In 2014, a statue of British and German soldiers shaking hands during the Christmas Day Truce was installed in Belgium.

enlisted athletes returned. Former Washington Senators outfielder Elmer J. Gedeon became a pilot in the US Army Air Forces. He died over France in 1944. Harry M. O'Neill of the Philadelphia Athletics was killed a year later in fierce fighting on the island of Iwo Jima in the Pacific Ocean.

Close to one thousand NFL players, coaches, and referees went to war in the 1940s. The player shortage became so severe that in 1943, the Pittsburgh Steelers and Philadelphia Eagles agreed to a one-year merger. They called themselves the Steagles. Then the Steelers merged with the Chicago Cardinals to form the Card-Pitt Combine. The team was a disaster, losing all of the games it played in 1944.

Pro sports continued during the war, but with so many top male athletes at war, the talent pool was thin. Retired players returned to fill rosters. Less talented players who would usually not make pro teams got the opportunity to play. Women also had the opportunity to play in roles usually held by men.

The Steagles beat the Washington Redskins 27–14 on November 28, 1943, at Griffith Stadium in Washington, DC.

Meanwhile, sports provided rare glimpses of hope to those fighting in war. Prisoners of war often faced dismal conditions in World War II. Some Allied soldiers in German prisoner-of-war camps played soccer and other sports to help pass the time. Soldiers also turned to sports for distraction from the grim reality of war. They often played on muddy ground that had only recently served as a battlefield.

Ali Takes a Stand

Muhammad Ali had risen through the boxing ranks under his birth name, Cassius Clay. He converted to Islam in 1964 and changed his name. In 1966, Ali was the world heavyweight boxing champion and one of the biggest stars in sports.

US involvement in the Vietnam War (1954–1975) was intensifying at the time. The United States backed the government of South Vietnam in the bloody conflict. The USSR, a former group of fifteen republics including Russia, supported North Vietnam. The United States and the USSR had been engaged in the Cold War (1945–1991) for decades. The sides were hostile to each other but avoided open war. Many US citizens saw the fighting in Vietnam as an extension of the Cold War and felt the conflict was unjust.

Young men were being drafted into the US armed forces to fight and die in Vietnam. Ali was selected for service and ordered to report for duty in April 1967. He refused. Ali stated that he had no reason to fight the Viet Cong, the North Vietnam forces that the US was fighting. He said that as a Muslim he was a pacifist and would only go to war if Allah (the Muslim word for God) ordered it. Ali applied for and was denied official status as a person morally opposed to the war.

Ali may not have been at risk of facing combat. With his celebrity status, the US military might have just used him to improve public opinions about the war. Yet Ali was strongly against the fighting in Vietnam. He was prepared to do whatever it took to avoid taking part in it. When he formally refused to enter service on April 28, 1967, he knew what would happen.

Two months later, the US military formally charged Ali with the crime of draft evasion. He was sentenced to five years in prison, fined $10,000, and stripped of his passport and his boxing titles.

In his first fight after his ban from boxing, Ali (*left*) beat Jerry Quarry on October 26, 1970.

He suddenly stood at the center of a growing debate over the conflict. The Vietnam War was increasingly unpopular in the United States. Ali's refusal to serve became a symbol of the growing resistance to the fighting. Some hailed him as a hero who stood up for the rights of young men—especially people of color and people with low income and social status who made up the great majority of draftees. Others branded him a coward.

Ali could have fled to Canada to avoid prison. He refused to do that as well. "America is my home," he said. "Do you think I would let somebody chase me out of my home? Nobody is going to chase me out of my birthplace. If they say I have to go to jail, then I will. But I'm not gonna run away, and you should know it."

Ali was in the prime of his career, but he was banned from the boxing ring. So he took his fight to the courts. He fought his case all the way to the US Supreme Court. Eventually, his sentence was overturned and his ban ended. After three years out of the ring, Ali returned in 1970 and went on to regain his world title. He is widely thought of as the greatest heavyweight boxer ever despite losing three years of his career standing up against a war he believed was wrong.

A Patriotic Outlet

Sports in the United States have served as outlets for protest against war, but people also use sports as platforms to express patriotism.

On January 27, 1991, the Buffalo Bills and the New York Giants took the field for Super Bowl XXV. It was just ten days after the US became involved in the first Gulf War (1990–1991) in Iraq and Kuwait. Iraq had invaded neighboring Kuwait in the summer of 1990. The US military and its allies invaded the region to protect Kuwait. Feelings of patriotism were running higher than they had in decades. Yet fears of a terrorist attack at the game made people uneasy. Security at the stadium in Tampa, Florida, was high as pop star Whitney Houston stepped onto the field to sing the national anthem.

It was a moment to remember. Houston belted out the "Star Spangled Banner" in a way few had ever heard. Backed by an orchestra, Houston took the upbeat anthem and slowed it down, filling it with emotion. Fans at the stadium and at home hung on every note. Four US military F-16 fighter jets zoomed overhead as the song ended. Houston's vocals tapped into a deep well of patriotism in a way that few singers of the anthem had ever done before.

A decade later, another wave of intense patriotism followed the terrorist attacks of September 11, 2001. The devastating attacks on New York City and Washington, DC, left Americans shaken. The skies were closed to air traffic for days. Baseball and football stadiums stood empty as games were put on hold. Racetracks were silent. When was the right time to resume playing?

Houston once said of her national anthem performance, "A lot of our daughters and sons were overseas fighting. I could see, in the stadium, I could see the fear, the hope, the intensity, the prayers going up. And I just felt, 'This is the moment.'"

Everyone had an opinion. Games were not important, some said. Others argued that sports were needed more than ever to help bring a sense of relief to a nation that was still in mourning.

The baseball season resumed about a week later. American flags were out in force in ballparks around the nation. Fans and players wept as singers performed the national anthem. In the first game played in New York following the September 11 attacks, Mets catcher Mike Piazza belted an eighth-inning home run to power his team past the Atlanta Braves. A few months later, the fittingly named New England Patriots won the Super Bowl.

Moments like these stand as a reminder that sports are part of the US national identity. They have a unique ability to bring people together. Sports can promote unity and help people heal from tragedy.

From the NFL to the Front Lines

Arizona Cardinals defender Pat Tillman was entering his fourth season in the NFL when the terror attacks of September 11, 2001, sent shock waves around the United States. He was coming off a 2000 season in which he made 109 tackles for the Cardinals. Scouts saw him as a rising defensive star in the NFL.

The terrorism affected Tillman deeply. He spoke about his feelings a day after the attacks. He mentioned his great-grandfather who served at Pearl Harbor during World War II. He talked about other family members who had served in the military. Tillman said he felt a calling to follow in their footsteps and serve in the US military.

Many athletes and public figures expressed similar feelings after the September 11 attacks. But the idea of serving in the US military was especially important to Tillman. He set out to do something about it. After the 2001 NFL season, Tillman turned down a multi-million-dollar contract offer from the Cardinals. Just as he was about to enter the best years of his playing career, he walked away from the NFL. Along with his brother Kevin, a minor-league baseball player, Tillman joined the US Army.

It was a stunning decision. While his former NFL teammates went to training camp to prepare for the 2002 season, Tillman went to boot camp to become a soldier. He and Kevin became US Army Rangers. They went to Afghanistan as a part of Operation Enduring Freedom. The mission's goal

Tillman (*right*), shown in this 2002 photo, served in both Iraq and Afghanistan.

was to overthrow the Taliban government that controlled Afghanistan and that was suspected of protecting terrorists.

On April 22, 2004, Tillman was on patrol in Sperah, Afghanistan. He was killed by friendly fire in a tragic accident. He became the first NFL player killed in active duty since the Vietnam War. To honor Tillman, the Cardinals retired his number-40 jersey so no other Arizona player could ever wear it. The US government awarded him the Purple Heart and Silver Star, two of the military's highest honors.

Approximately 3,500 people attended a memorial service for Tillman on May 3, 2004, at the San Jose Municipal Rose Garden. Sports TV and radio host Jim Rome (*at podium*) and others spoke during the service.

COMING TOGETHER

On April 15, 2013, runners and fans gathered for the Boston Marathon. The yearly event is one of the biggest races in the world. As runners neared the finish line, terrorists Tamerlan and Dzhokhar Tsarnaev set off an explosion near the marathon's route. The blast killed three people and injured hundreds more. It left the usually peaceful marathon route looking like a war zone.

Boston and the nation rallied around the disaster. Five days later, the Boston Red Sox held their first home game since the attack. Boston superstar David Ortiz walked to the middle of the field and grabbed a microphone before the game started. He gave a brief but moving speech. He told fans not to give in to fear. "This jersey that we wear today, it doesn't say 'Red Sox,'" he said. "It says 'Boston'. . . . This is our . . . city. And nobody's going to dictate our freedom. Stay strong."

The crowd roared. Boston police official Ed Davis was at the game and heard Ortiz's speech. He said that Ortiz spoke aloud what was on many people's minds that day. "He was a guy that just sort of spoke for all of Boston," Davis said.

Ortiz holds a Boston Strong sign, which honors the marathon bombing victims.

57

Basketball player LeBron James often speaks up about his political views. Journalist Laura Ingraham told James to "shut up and dribble." James responded by naming his 2018 NBA documentary series *Shut Up and Dribble*.

CONCLUSION

SPORTS CULTURE

Sports have long mirrored a culture of exclusion in the United States. Minorities and women have been seen as second-class citizens in US society. That mindset is reflected in sports. In recent years, progress toward a more open society has been steady, if sometimes slow. Sports have grown more welcoming to people of all races and gender identities. And athletes have come to recognize and embrace the role of sports in culture. Many have used their voices to drive social change.

The past century has seen a gradual progression toward greater inclusivity in sports for all people. While racial tensions still exist in sports and society, athletes of color are free to compete on the same field in the United States. The right for women to play the same sports as men has made tremendous strides, and women's team sports are quickly gaining popularity. Meanwhile, gay and transgender athletes continue to make gains in the battle for inclusion.

Sports have always been a reflection of the culture that nurtures them. People who are oppressed in society are likewise oppressed in sports. Social change can be measured—and even foretold—by changes in the culture of sports. When sports and culture collide, they can help to spur change, raise awareness, and even alter the way people think about one another.

SOURCE NOTES

6   Cindy Boren, "Colin Kaepernick Reportedly Will Now Stand During the National Anthem," *The Washington Post*, March 2, 2017, https://www.washingtonpost.com/news/early-lead/wp/2017/03/02/colin-kaepernick-reportedly-will-now-stand-during-the-national-anthem/?utm_term=.bb0de5097ba8.

10   John Ridley, "A True Champion Vs. The 'Great White Hope,' " NPR, July 2, 2010, https://www.npr.org/templates/story/story.php?storyId=128245468.

12   Larry Schwartz, "Owens Pierced a Myth," ESPN, accessed October 1, 2018, https://web.archive.org/web/20000815053753/http://espn.go.com:80/sportscentury/features/00016393.html.

15   "Newk: Why It Had to Be Jackie," Fox Sports, April 10, 2013, http://www.foxsports.com/mlb/story/don-newcombe-tells-why-jackie-robinson-was-right-man-to-integrate-major-league-baseball-041013.

20   Frank Fitzpatrick, "Texas Western's 1966 Title Left Lasting Legacy," ESPN, November 19, 2003, https://espn.go.com/classic/s/013101_texas_western_fitzpatrick.html.

23   DeNeen L. Brown, "They Didn't #TakeTheKnee: The Black Power Protest Salute that Shook the World in 1968," *The Washington Post*, September 24, 2017, https://www.washingtonpost.com/news/retropolis/wp/2017/09/24/they-didnt-takeaknee-the-black-power-protest-salute-that-shook-the-world-in-1968/?noredirect=on&utm_term=.dfdcb9cd2a93.

23   Ibid.

23   David Davis, "Olympic Athletes Who Took a Stand," *Smithsonian*, August 2008, https://www.smithsonianmag.com/articles/olympic-athletes-who-took-a-stand-593920.

27   Austin Knoblauch, "Roger Goodell Doesn't See Redskins Name Change," NFL, January 30, 2018, http://www.nfl.com/news/story/0ap3000000912193/article/roger-goodell-doesnt-see-redskins-name-change.

29   Les Carpenter, "Ibtihaj Muhammad's Bronze: A Vital US Medal in this Summer of Trump," *The Guardian*, August 13, 2016, https://www.theguardian.com/sport/2016/aug/13/ibtihaj-muhammad-fencing-olympics-2016-bronze.

30   Kent Babb, "The Making of Colin Kaepernick," *Washington Post*, September 7, 2017, https://www.washingtonpost.com/sports/the-making-of-colin-kaepernick/2017/09/07/d4d58e20-9320-11e7-8754-d478688d23b4_story.html?utm_term=.4e05570356c0.

30   Chris Minor, "Knox College Lifts Suspension for Player's Ferguson Protest," WQAD, December 2, 2014, https://wqad.com/2014/12/02/knox-college-lifts-suspension-in-ferguson-protest-on-basketball-court.

33   Jeva Lange, "Why on Earth Does the Olympics Still Refer to Hundreds of Athletes as 'Ladies'?," *The Week*, February 9, 2018, http://theweek.com/articles/754038/why-earth-does-olympics-still-refer-hundreds-athletes-ladies.

36   Larry Schwartz, "Billie Jean Won for All Women," ESPN, accessed October 1, 2018, https://www.espn.com/sportscentury/features/00016060.html.

36   Johnette Howard, "Twelve Years Later, Still the Best," ESPN, June 23, 2011, http://www.espn.com/espn/commentary/news/story?page=howard-110623.

40   John Branch, "N.F.L. Prospect Michael Sam Proudly Says What Teammates Knew: He's Gay," *The New York Times*, February 9, 2014, https://www.nytimes.com/2014/02/10/sports/michael-sam-college-football-star-says-he-is-gay-ahead-of-nfl-draft.html.

40   Wendy Liberatore, "First Openly Gay NFL Player Shares Story," *Times Union*, February 9, 2017, https://www.timesunion.com/sports/article/First-openly-gay-NFL-player-shares-story-10916280.php.

43   Jos Truitt, "Fallon Fox on Life as a Trans Athlete: 'The Scope of Vitriol and Anger was Mind-Blowing,' " *The Guardian* (US), February 16, 2015, http://www.theguardian.com/sport/2015/feb/16/fallon-fox-trans-mma-athlete-interview.

44   "'Sister Survivors' of Larry Nassar's Sexual Abuse Honored with Arthur Ashe Courage Award," ESPN, July 19, 2018, http://www.espn.com/espys/story/_/id/24134624/2018-espys-arthur-ashe-courage-award-goes-survivors-larry-nassar-sexual-abuse.

44   Juliet Macur, "The 'Me Too' Movement Inevitably Spills Into Sports," *The New York Times*, October 19, 2017, https://www.nytimes.com/2017/10/19/sports/olympics/mckayla-maroney-me-too.html.

52   Jerry Izenberg, "Muhammad Ali: Why They Called Him 'The Greatest' and Why I Called Him My Friend," *NJ*, June 4, 2016, http://www.nj.com/sports/index.ssf/2016/06/former_heavyweight_champ_muhammad_ali_dies_the_gre.html.

53   Jordan Runtagh, "Heal the World: 20 Songs for a Good Cause," *Rolling Stone*, November 22, 2018, https://www.rollingstone.com/music/music-lists/benefit-concerts-songs-good-cause-geldof-live-aid-720175/the-star-spangled-banner-sung-by-whitney-houston-1991-722486/

57   Scott Lauber, "David Ortiz's finest moment with the Red Sox wasn't at the plate," ESPN, April 10, 2016, http://www.espn.com/mlb/story/_/id/15175959/david-ortiz-finest-moment-red-sox-plate.

57   Ibid.

GLOSSARY

boycott: an organized refusal to interact with a product or group for political reasons

Civil Right Act: a US law passed in 1964 that bans segregation in public places such as schools and businesses

civil rights movement: the fight in the 1950s and 1960s to end discrimination and segregation in the United States

fencing: a sport in which two competitors fight with swords, scoring points for touching the opponent with the weapons' blunted tips

hijab: a traditional Muslim head covering worn by women

integration: the process of including people who were previously segregated

pacifist: a person with a moral objection to war

preseason: games and practices that take place before the start of the regular season, and which don't count in the standings

prime: the most productive years of an athlete's career

scholarship: money awarded to help pay for education expenses

scout: a person who evaluates athletic talent and helps teams make decisions about players to draft or sign

segregation: the forced separation of different racial or ethnic groups

transgender: a person whose gender identity does not match their identity at birth

SELECTED BIBLIOGRAPHY

Branch, John. "The Awakening of Colin Kaepernick." *The New York Times*. September 7, 2017, https://www.nytimes.com/2017/09/07/sports/colin-kaepernick-nfl-protests.html.

Branch, John. "N.F.L. Prospect Michael Sam Proudly Says What Teammates Knew: He's Gay." *The New York Times*. February 9, 2014, https://www.nytimes.com/2014/02/10/sports/michael-sam-college-football-star-says-he-is-gay-ahead-of-nfl-draft.html.

Brown, DeNeen L. "They Didn't #TakeTheKnee: The Black Power Protest Salute that Shook the World in 1968." *The Washington Post*. September 14, 2017, https://www.washingtonpost.com/news/retropolis/wp/2017/09/24/they-didnt-takeaknee-the-black-power-protest-salute-that-shook-the-world-in-1968/?noredirect=on&utm_term=.dfdcb9cd2a93.

Doeden, Matt. *Muhammad Ali: The Greatest*. Minneapolis: Lerner Publications, 2017.

Macur, Juliet. "The 'Me Too' Movement Inevitably Spills Into Sports." *The New York Times*. October 19, 2017, https://www.nytimes.com/2017/10/19/sports/olympics/mckayla-maroney-me-too.html.

Rappaport, Doreen. *42 Is Not Just a Number: The Odyssey of Jackie Robinson, American Hero*. Somerville: Candlewick Press, 2017.

FURTHER READING

Cronn-Mills, Kirstin. *LGBTQ+ Athletes Claim the Field*. Minneapolis: Twenty-First Century Books, 2017.

Doeden, Matt. *The Negro Leagues: Celebrating Baseball's Unsung Heroes*. Minneapolis: Millbrook Press, 2017.

ESPN: Significant Moments in Sports and War
http://www.espn.com/page2/s/list/warandsports.html

Koya, Lena, and Laura La Bella. *Female Athletes*. New York: Rosen, 2018.

Leigh, Anna. *Aly Raisman: Athlete and Activist*. Minneapolis: Lerner Publications, 2019.

PBS: Civil Rights Movement (1954–1985)
http://www.pbs.org/black-culture/explore/civil-rights-movement/#.WzGvSadKjIU

SBNation: Everything You Need to Know about NFL Protests During the National Anthem
https://www.sbnation.com/2017/9/29/16380080/donald-trump-nfl-colin-kaepernick-protests-national-anthem

INDEX

ABOUT THE AUTHOR

Matt Doeden began his career as a sportswriter, covering everything from high school sports to the NFL. Since then he has written hundreds of children's and young adult books on topics ranging from history to sports to current events. His book *Darkness Everywhere: The Assassination of Mohandas Gandhi* was listed among the Best Children's Books of the Year by the Children's Book Committee at Bank Street College. Doeden lives in Minnesota with his wife and two children.

PHOTO ACKNOWLEDGMENTS

The images in this book are used with the permission of: Harry How/Getty Images, p. 4; Thearon W. Henderson/Getty Images, p. 7; Philipp Kester/ullstein bild/Getty Images, p. 8; PA Images/Getty Images, p. 11; Associated Press, pp. 13, 19, 21 (top right); International News Photography/Sports Studio Photos/Getty Images, p. 15; Photo File/MLB Photos/Getty Images, p. 16; Bettmann/Getty Images, pp. 18, 21 (top left), 32, 46; Augusta National/Getty Images, p. 21 (middle left); Jamie-Andrea Yanak/Associated Press, p. 21 (middle right); Nick Cammett/Diamond Images/Getty Images, p. 21 (bottom right); RacingOne/ ISC Archives/Getty Images, p. 21 (bottom left); Popperfoto/Getty Images, p. 22; Chris Smith/Popperfoto/Getty Images, p. 24; Ann Heisenfelt/Associated Press, p. 26; Daniel Zuchnik/WireImage/Getty Images, p. 28; Michael Reaves/Getty Images, p. 31; AP Photo/Houston Chronicle, BLAIR PITTMAN, R00032313, p. 35; Jed Jacobsohn/Getty Images, p. 37; Stacy Revere/Getty Images, p. 39; Marc Serota/Getty Images, p. 41; Sally Ryan/zReportage.com via ZUMA Press, p. 42; Michael Caulfield/Associated Press, p. 43; Phil McCarten/Invision/Associated Press, p. 45; Arterra/UIG/Getty Images, p. 48; Nate Fine/NFL/Getty Images, p. 49; Paul Slade/Getty Images, p. 51; George Rose/Getty Images, p. 53; Columbus Ledger-Enquirer/Getty Images, p. 55; David Paul Morris/Getty Images, p. 56; Jim Rogash/Getty Images, p. 57; Steve Dykes/Getty Images, p. 58

Front cover: Focus On Sport/Getty Images (top), Michael Zagaris/Getty Images (bottom). Back cover: Ezra Shaw/Getty Images. Flap: Sports Studio Photos/Getty Images

.75

Thanksgiving

FESTIVE RECIPES
FOR THE HOLIDAY TABLE

GENERAL EDITOR
CHUCK WILLIAMS

RECIPES
KRISTINE KIDD

PHOTOGRAPHY
ALLAN ROSENBERG

TIME
LIFE
BOOKS

TIME-LIFE BOOKS

Time-Life Books is a division of Time Life Inc.

Time-Life is a trademark of Time Warner Inc. U.S.A.

Time-Life Custom Publishing
Vice President of Sales and Marketing: Neil Levin
Director of Financial Operations: J. Brian Birky
Director of Acquisitions: Jennifer L. Pearce

WILLIAMS-SONOMA
Founder and Vice Chairman: Chuck Williams
Associate Book Buyer: Cecilia Michaelis

WELDON OWEN INC.
Chief Executive Officer: John Owen
President: Terry Newell
Vice President and Publisher: Wendely Harvey
Chief Operating Officer: Larry Partington
Vice President International Sales: Stuart Laurence
Managing Editor: Lisa Chaney Atwood
Project Coordinator: Judith Dunham
Consulting Editor: Norman Kolpas
Copy Editor: Sharon Silva
Design: John Bull, The Book Design Company
Production Director: Stephanie Sherman
Production Manager: Jen Dalton
Production Editor: Sarah Lemas
Food Photographer: Allan Rosenberg
Additional Food Photography: Allen V. Lott
Food Stylist: Heidi Gintner
Prop Stylist: Sandra Griswold
Assistant Food Stylist: Kim Konecny
Glossary Illustrations: Alice Harth

The Williams-Sonoma Kitchen Library
conceived and produced by Weldon Owen Inc.
814 Montgomery St., San Francisco, CA 94133

In collaboration with Williams-Sonoma
3250 Van Ness Ave., San Francisco, CA 94109

Printed in China by Toppan Printing Co., LTD.

A Note on Weights and Measures:
All recipes include customary U.S. and metric measurements. Metric conversions are based on a standard developed for these books and have been rounded off. Actual weights may vary.

A Weldon Owen Production

Copyright © 1997 Williams-Sonoma and Weldon Owen Inc.
Reprinted in 1997; 1998; 1999; 2000
All rights reserved, including the right of reproduction in whole or in part in any form.

Library of Congress
Cataloging-in-Publication Data:

Kidd, Kristine.
    Thanksgiving / general editor, Chuck Williams ; recipes, Kristine Kidd; photography, Allan Rosenberg.
       p.   cm. — (Williams-Sonoma kitchen library)
    ISBN 0-7835-0324-5
    1. Thanksgiving cookery.   I. Williams, Chuck
II. Title.   III. Series.
    TX739.2.T45K53   1997
    641.5'68—dc21   96-29831
                                                      CIP

Contents

STARTERS 15

MAIN COURSES 35

STUFFINGS & SIDE DISHES 47

BREADS & DESSERTS 79

INTRODUCTION

Thanksgiving dinner has always been one of my favorite meals, as it offers an opportunity to gather with family and good friends around a festive holiday table. This book of Thanksgiving recipes aims to help you, the person who cooks the meal, enjoy the occasion as much as your guests will.

To that end, you'll find 49 recipes here for everything from soups and salads to whole roasted turkeys, cranberry sauces and gravies to irresistible quick breads and holiday desserts. Kristine Kidd's recipes come from America's heartland tradition, so even ingredients or preparations you never have served before will have a homey, familiar ring to them. You'll also notice that there are alternatives to the usual whole roasted turkey, in the event that you are looking to change the main attraction of your holiday meal.

Every one of the recipes has been kitchen-tested to make sure it will work easily and successfully for you. Introductory step-by-step instructions on choosing, roasting and carving a turkey and on making gravy, as well as menu-planning guidelines and a glossary of cooking terms and techniques, will help ensure that your next Thanksgiving dinner is the easiest you've ever prepared.

I urge you to spend some time in the week or so before Thanksgiving organizing your holiday meal. Read through the recipes you plan to make, jotting down shopping lists for ingredients, table decorations and any cooking equipment or serving pieces you might need. Give yourself plenty of time to do the shopping, then try to strategize the meal, from the moment guests arrive to the final cleanup. Prepare as many things in advance as time and space allow.

With some of the cooking and other preparations done ahead, you'll find yourself with more time to set a pretty table, and then to relax and enjoy the holiday meal with your guests.

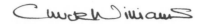

4

EQUIPMENT

Basic kitchen tools that help achieve successful results when preparing your Thanksgiving meal

Apart from advance planning, nothing will make the preparation of a Thanksgiving meal go quicker than having the right tools on hand. When you plan your menu, review the equipment you'll need to prepare, cook and serve each recipe, then arrange to borrow or buy anything you lack.

1. Mixing Bowls
For easy mixing, choose deep bowls in a range of sizes. Lips and handles facilitate pouring.

2. Muffin Tin
Tray of individual cups (about 3½ fl oz/110 ml) for baking standard-sized muffins. Whenever possible, choose a stick-resistant tin.

3. Baking Sheets
For baking pastries and toasting nuts. Select heavy aluminum or tinned steel. Dark, heavy-duty metal sheets conduct heat efficiently for fast, even browning.

4. Sieve
For all-purpose draining and straining.

5. Assorted Utensils
Crockery jar holds a metal ladle; wooden spoons; metal serving and slotted spoons; large and small wire whisks; rubber spatulas; basting and scrubbing brushes; and a potato masher.

6. Colander
For draining vegetables and fruits after washing and after cooking.

7. Liquid Measuring Cup
Choose heavy-duty, heat-resistant glass, marked on one side in cups and ounces and on the other in milliliters.

8. Sifter
For sifting dry ingredients in baking. Also used to sift confectioners' (icing) sugar to decorate desserts and baked goods.

9. Cutting Board
Choose a good-sized cutting board made of sturdy hardwood or tough but resilient white acrylic.

10. Biscuit Cutter
Stainless-steel tool cuts neat round biscuits and cookies.

11. Vegetable Peeler
Curved, slotted, swiveling blade thinly strips away peels.

12. Pie Server
Choose a utensil with a sturdy, wedge-shaped blade.

13. Kitchen Knives
Large and medium-sized chef's knives for chopping and slicing large items or quantities of food. Smaller paring knife for peeling vegetables and cutting up small ingredients.

14. Melon Ball Scoop
Sharp-edged stainless-steel scoop cuts neat spheres from soft fruits and vegetables.

carving knife cuts between poultry joints and slices meats with ease.

17. Carving Board
Hardwood board holds large roasts for easy carving and captures juices that flow from the meat as it is sliced.

18. Rolling Pin
Select a sturdy hardwood dowel-type pin for best control when rolling out pie or cookie dough.

19. Baking Pans
Small metal loaf pan for baking quick breads and cakes. Larger rectangular dish for all-purpose oven baking.

20. Saucepans
For making soups, gravies and small quantities of stock and for cooking vegetables.

21. Dutch Oven or Casserole
Large-capacity cooking vessel with tight-fitting lid, for use on the stove top or in the oven.

22. Wire Cooling Racks
Permit air to circulate under baked goods for even cooling.

23. Tart Pan
Removable bottom of standard 9-inch (23-cm) pan allows tart to be unmolded easily. Fluted sides give crust an attractive edge.

24. Springform Pan
Circular pan with high spring-clip sides that loosen easily for unmolding cakes.

25. Glass Pie Dish
Attractive container for baking and serving pie retains heat well for crisp, brown crusts.

26. Pot Holder
Heavy-duty cotton provides protection from hot cookware.

27. Kitchen String
For trussing poultry, good-quality linen string withstands intense heat.

28. Instant-Read Thermometer
Provides quick, accurate measure of internal temperature when inserted into the thickest part of the item being cooked.

29. Trussing Pins
Flexible metal pins with hooked ends, used to close up the cavity of poultry before roasting.

30. Measuring Spoons
In graduated sizes, for measuring small quantities of dry or liquid ingredients.

31. Dry Measuring Cups
For accurate measuring of dry ingredients, choose good-quality calibrated metal cups in graduated sizes, with straight rims that allow for leveling.

32. Roasting Pan and Rack
Heavy, durable metal pan large enough to hold roasts. Sturdy metal rack promotes even cooking and prevents sticking.

15. Bulb Baster
Stainless-steel tube and rubber bulb efficiently and safely suction up pan juices for basting.

16. Carving Fork and Knife
Sturdy two-pronged fork steadies roasts, while the long, sharp, flexible blade of a

Turkey Basics

Most Thanksgiving dinners feature a whole roast turkey. For the best flavor and texture, seek out a farm-fresh, ready-to-cook bird with creamy white to creamy yellow skin that looks moist and supple and has well-distributed fat. You can also get satisfactory results from a frozen turkey. Just be sure to allow ample time for it to defrost completely in the refrigerator before cooking, following the guidelines on the package.

Selecting the Right Pan

For the best results, roast the turkey on a wire roasting rack set inside a sturdy, open pan (see page 7). The turkey will be easier to handle if the pan is proportionate to the bird's size. For a turkey that weighs 10–14 pounds (5–7 kg), use a pan measuring 14 by 10 by 2½ inches (35 by 25 by 6 cm); for 16–20 pounds (8–10 kg), a pan measuring 17 by 11½ by 2½ inches (43 by 29 by 6 cm); for 24 pounds (12 kg) and over, a pan measuring 19 by 14 by 3¼ inches (48 by 35 by 9 cm).

Roasting Times and Temperatures

All roasting times given in this book are for a room-temperature turkey. To bring your turkey to room temperature, remove it from the refrigerator 1–1½ hours before roasting. Do not leave it out for longer.

For an unstuffed bird, figure on a roasting time of 13–15 minutes per pound (500 g). If you've stuffed the turkey, add 30 minutes to the total cooking time for a bird up to 16 pounds (8 kg) or up to 1 hour for a larger turkey. This timing is based on roasting the turkey at a temperature of 325°F (165°C).

Testing for Doneness

About 30 minutes before the estimated total roasting time is reached, insert an instant-read thermometer (see page 7) into the thickest part of the breast, and then the thigh, without touching the bone. The breast should reach at least 170°F (77°C) and the thigh 180°F (82°C). Do not leave the thermometer in the turkey while it roasts. The breast will be done before the thigh; to stop its skin from overbrowning during the final minutes of roasting, cover it with aluminum foil, placed shiny side out.

A turkey will continue to cook internally after you remove it from the oven, so you may take it out when the temperature is 3–4°F (1–2°C) below the minimums given above. Cover the bird loosely with foil and let it rest for 20 minutes before carving.

To Stuff or Not to Stuff

Roasting a bird unstuffed, with a separately baked dressing, saves effort and time, and a dressing baked outside the bird contains none of the additional fat that it would absorb inside the turkey. For many people, however, a stuffed bird is traditional. If you prefer your turkey stuffed, spoon the prepared mixture loosely into the body and neck cavities just before roasting and truss the body opening. A stuffing must also be tested for doneness and should register an internal temperature of 160°F (71°C) on an instant-read thermometer. Remove all of the stuffing at serving time, and transfer it to a warmed dish.

ROASTING A TURKEY

Two important keys to a well-browned bird with moist meat are trussing it to keep its shape more compact and basting it regularly.

1. Rinsing the turkey.
Check the body and neck cavities and remove the neck and any packaged giblets inside. Rinse the bird inside and out with cold running water and pat dry with paper towels. With your fingers, pull out and discard any pieces of fat from the cavities.

2. Stuffing the turkey.
If you choose to stuff the turkey, use a large spoon or your hands to transfer the prepared stuffing, packing it loosely into the body and neck cavities. Do not overfill, as the stuffing expands while the turkey roasts. Rub the turkey with any seasonings called for in the recipe.

3. Trussing the turkey.
To secure the stuffing, pass several trussing pins through the skin on both sides of the main cavity. Cut a generous length of kitchen string and, starting at the topmost pin, interlace the string back and forth as you would shoelaces. Pull it snug and tie it securely at the bottom.

4. Securing the drumsticks and wings.
Transfer the turkey to a rack in a roasting pan. Cut a piece of string about 10 inches (25 cm) long. Cross the drumsticks, wind the string around the drumsticks and tie the ends tightly. Tuck the wing tips under the body.

5. Basting the turkey.
At intervals specified in individual recipes, use a large spoon or a bulb baster to collect the pan juices and pour them evenly over the entire turkey. About 30 minutes before the estimated roasting time, start testing for doneness.

Herb-Rubbed Turkey with Mushroom Gravy

MAKING GRAVY

Simply and quickly prepared from the juices left in the roasting pan, gravy is a rich addition to the Thanksgiving turkey and its accompaniments. Using aromatic vegetables, herbs and flavorful liquids lets you make gravies of appealing variety.

1. Skimming off the fat.
Pour the juices from the roasting pan into a measuring pitcher. Using a large, flat spoon, skim off and discard the layer of fat floating on top. Add enough additional stock or other liquids to reach the desired measure.

2. Stirring in the stock.
Heat fat—here, butter—and sauté aromatics, in this case sliced shallots and chopped fresh thyme. Add flour and cook, stirring frequently, until it has browned. Then, gradually whisk in the stock mixture.

3. Thickening the gravy.
Bring the mixture to a boil, whisking frequently. Continue boiling, stirring occasionally, until thickened. For more flavor, whisk in a little brandy or other liqueur, or cream, and return to a boil before serving.

CARVING A TURKEY

When the turkey is done, transfer it to a carving board and let it rest, covered loosely with aluminum foil, for 20 minutes. Use a good, sharp carving knife and a two-pronged fork to carve one side of the turkey before starting on the other.

1. Removing the leg and wing.
With the turkey breast up, cut through the skin between the thigh and breast. Move the leg to locate the thigh joint, then cut through the joint to sever the leg. In the same way, remove the wing, cutting through the shoulder joint where it meets the breast.

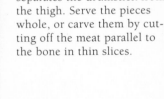

2. Slicing the drumstick and thigh.
Cut through the joint that separates the drumstick from the thigh. Serve the pieces whole, or carve them by cutting off the meat parallel to the bone in thin slices.

3. Carving the breast.
Just above the thigh and shoulder joints, carve a deep horizontal cut toward the bone, creating a base cut on one side of the breast. Starting near the breastbone, carve thin slices vertically, cutting parallel to the rib cage and ending each slice at the base cut.

CREATING A MENU

The four menus below suggest the many different combinations you can compose using the recipes in this book and adjusting the quantities to accommodate the number of guests at your holiday meal. The varied menus follow some common guidelines. One or more light appetizers whet the palate for the hearty main course. Traditional accompaniments include cranberry sauce, a fresh vegetable, potatoes or yams, and a quick bread. Dessert hews to richly spiced autumn favorites.

✢ An Elegant Dinner ✢

Smoked Salmon Toasts
Brandied Chestnut Soup
Cider-Glazed Turkey with Cider-Shallot Gravy
Caramelized Onion and Mushroom Stuffing
Mashed Potatoes with Basil and Chives
Brussels Sprouts with Orange Butter and Hazelnuts
Lemon and Molasses Whole-Wheat Biscuits
Cranberry Sauce with Grapefruit and Honey
Cashew, Almond and Walnut Caramel Tart

✢ Vegetarian Dinner ✢

Rosemary and Spice Nuts
Endive, Fennel and Walnut Salad
Roasted Fall Vegetables with Wild Rice Pilaf
Orange, Walnut and Pear Pumpkin Bread
Cranberry Sauce with Mustard
Apple Pie with Lemon and Vanilla

✢ Dinner for a Small Gathering ✢

Green Bean, Caramelized Onion and Blue Cheese Salad
Roast Turkey Breast with Rosemary-Mustard Butter
Dried Fruit, Nut and Apple Stuffing
Mashed Potatoes, Rutabagas and Sautéed Leeks
Herbed Corn Bread
Cranberry, Pear and Orange Relish
Ginger-Molasses Pumpkin Pie

✢ Dinner with Baked Ham ✢

Spiced Apple, Cranberry and Pecan Salad
Baked Ham with Apricot-Mustard Glaze
Mashed Yams with Brown Sugar and Spice
Creamed Turnips and Chard
Spoonbread
Chive Cream Biscuits
Pear Upside-down Spice Cake

Turkey Stock

Using canned broth and extra necks results in a full-flavored stock. It can be refrigerated for up to 3 days.

1 tablespoon vegetable oil
1 lb (500 g) turkey necks, rinsed and cut into 2-inch (5-cm) pieces
1 large yellow onion, chopped
2 celery stalks with leaves, chopped
1 cup (8 fl oz/250 ml) dry white wine
7 cups (56 fl oz/1.75 l) canned low-sodium chicken broth or water
giblets from 1 turkey, excluding the liver, rinsed
6 peppercorns
2 bay leaves
5 fresh parsley sprigs

*I*n a large saucepan over high heat, warm the oil. Add the turkey necks; cook until browned on all sides, about 8 minutes. Add the onion and celery; cook until browned, about 15 minutes. Add the liquids and giblets. Bring to a simmer, skimming any foam from the surface. Add the peppercorns, bay leaves and parsley and bring to a boil. Reduce the heat to low, cover partially and simmer for 2 hours. Strain the stock through a fine-mesh sieve into a bowl. Discard the solids. Refrigerate the cooled stock in an airtight container. Before using, lift off the fat from the surface and discard.

Makes about 6 cups (48 fl oz/1.5 l)

Cranberry, Pear and Orange Relish

A touch of cardamom lends subtle spice to this zesty relish. It keeps fresh in the refrigerator for up to 3 days, so make it a few days before serving to save time on Thanksgiving morning.

1 thin-skinned orange with skin intact, cut into 8 wedges
1 bag (12 oz/375 g) cranberries (about 3 cups)
¾ cup (6 oz/185 g) sugar, or to taste
½ teaspoon ground cardamom
2 firm but ripe pears, peeled, quartered, cored and finely chopped

*U*sing the tip of a knife, remove any seeds from the orange wedges, then cut each wedge in half crosswise. Combine half of the orange pieces, cranberries and sugar in a food processor fitted with the metal blade. Process until finely chopped. Alternatively, using a blender, process until finely chopped. Transfer the mixture to a bowl. Repeat with the remaining orange pieces, cranberries and sugar. Add to the bowl.

Add the cardamom and pears to the cranberry mixture and stir to mix well. Taste and add more sugar, if desired. Cover and refrigerate until well chilled before serving.

Makes about 4 cups (2 lb/1 kg)

Cranberry Sauce with Mustard

Based on an old farm recipe for mustard pickles, this tart condiment is terrific with turkey or ham. It will keep in the refrigerator for up to 1 week.

1½ cups (12 oz/375 g) sugar
½ cup (4 fl oz/125 ml) cider vinegar
¼ cup (2 fl oz/60 ml) water
1 tablespoon dry mustard
½ teaspoon celery seeds
¼ teaspoon ground turmeric
¼ teaspoon salt
1 bag (12 oz/375 g) cranberries (about 3 cups)

*I*n a heavy saucepan, combine the sugar, vinegar, water, mustard, celery seeds, turmeric and salt. Whisk to dissolve the mustard. Bring to a boil over medium-high heat, stirring until the sugar dissolves. Add the cranberries and bring to a boil again. Reduce the heat to medium and boil gently, stirring occasionally, until the cranberries pop, about 10 minutes. Remove from the heat and let cool to room temperature. Transfer to a bowl, cover and refrigerate until well chilled before serving.

Makes about 2⅓ cups (1⅓ lb/655 g)

Cranberry Sauce with Grapefruit and Honey

Grapefruit, honey and ginger contribute new accents to a traditional sauce. This keeps well, so make it a few days before the meal.

1 bag (12 oz/375 g) cranberries (about 3 cups)
1 tablespoon grated grapefruit zest
1 cup (8 fl oz/250 ml) fresh grapefruit juice
¾ cup (9 oz/280 g) honey
⅓ cup (2 oz/60 g) minced crystallized ginger

*I*n a heavy saucepan over medium-high heat, combine the cranberries, grapefruit zest and juice and honey. Bring to a boil, stirring frequently. Boil, stirring occasionally, until the cranberries pop, about 5 minutes. Remove from the heat and let cool to room temperature. Stir in the crystallized ginger. Transfer to a bowl, cover and refrigerate until well chilled before serving.

Makes about 2¾ cups (1¾ lb/875 g)

Green Bean, Caramelized Onion and Blue Cheese Salad

salt

2½ lb (1.25 kg) green beans, stem ends trimmed

½ cup (4 fl oz/125 ml) plus 2 tablespoons olive oil

3 tablespoons plus 2 teaspoons sherry vinegar

2 tablespoons chopped fresh thyme or 2 teaspoons dried thyme

2 teaspoons soy sauce

1 teaspoon sugar

freshly ground pepper

3 large red (Spanish) onions, cut through stem ends into wedges ⅓–½-inch (9–12 mm) thick

1 cup (5 oz/155 g) crumbled blue cheese

Here is a stylish way to begin Thanksgiving dinner. The salad is equally good with fresh goat cheese. To make the party preparations easier, ready the beans and dressing and the onions early in the day, then assemble the salad just before serving.

*P*reheat a broiler (griller). Brush a baking sheet with oil.

Fill a large pot three-fourths full with water, salt it lightly and bring to a boil over high heat. Add the beans and boil until tender-crisp, about 5 minutes. Drain, rinse with cold water and drain well.

In a small bowl, whisk together the olive oil, vinegar, thyme, soy sauce and sugar until well blended. Season to taste with salt and pepper.

Arrange the onion wedges on the prepared baking sheet. Brush with some of the vinaigrette. Slip under the broiler about 3 inches (7.5 cm) from the heat source. Broil (grill) the onions, without turning, until deep brown, 8–12 minutes.

Place the beans in a large bowl. Add the remaining dressing and toss to coat. Divide the beans evenly among individual plates. Top with the onions, dividing evenly. Drizzle any dressing remaining at the bottom of the bowl over the onions. Sprinkle evenly with the cheese and serve.

Serves 8–10

Spiced Apple, Cranberry and Pecan Salad

1½ teaspoons ground cumin
¼ teaspoon cayenne pepper
1 tablespoon olive oil
1 cup (4 oz/125 g) pecan halves
3 tablespoons sugar
½ cup (4 oz/125 g) plain yogurt
½ cup (4 fl oz/125 ml) light mayonnaise
2 tablespoons honey
1 teaspoon sherry wine vinegar or
   balsamic vinegar
5 large sweet apples such as Gala,
   Golden Delicious or Fuji
3 large celery stalks, thinly sliced
½ cup (2 oz/60 g) dried cranberries
8–10 red leaf lettuce leaves

Caramelized pecans and dried cranberries, along with cumin and cayenne pepper, add new twists to the Waldorf salad. The light yogurt-based dressing makes it a refreshing start to the traditional turkey supper.

In a bowl, combine ¾ teaspoon of the cumin and ⅛ teaspoon of the cayenne pepper. Pour the oil into a small saucepan and place over medium heat until warm. Add the pecans and stir until the nuts are light brown, about 5 minutes. Sprinkle with the sugar and cook, stirring constantly, until the sugar melts and begins to brown, about 3 minutes. Add the hot nut mixture to the bowl holding the spices and stir to coat. Let cool completely. Chop the nuts coarsely. Set aside.

In a small bowl, stir together the yogurt, mayonnaise, honey and vinegar, and the remaining ¾ teaspoon cumin and ⅛ teaspoon cayenne pepper.

Quarter each apple through the stem end and cut away the core. Cut each quarter in half crosswise, then slice. In a large bowl, combine the apples, celery and dried cranberries. Add the yogurt dressing and toss to coat.

Line individual plates with lettuce leaves. Mound an equal amount of the salad in the center of each plate. Sprinkle with the nuts and serve.

Serves 8–10

Wild Mushroom Soup

10 oz (315 g) fresh wild mushrooms such as chanterelle, oyster and/or shiitake
12 oz (375 g) fresh cultivated white mushrooms
5 tablespoons (2½ oz/75 g) butter
12 shallots, sliced
3 leeks, white part and 1 inch (2.5 cm) of the green, halved lengthwise, carefully rinsed and sliced crosswise
¼ cup (1½ oz/45 g) all-purpose (plain) flour
5 cups (40 fl oz/1.25 l) beef stock or canned low-sodium broth
5 cups (40 fl oz/1.25 l) chicken stock or canned low-sodium broth
2½ tablespoons chopped fresh tarragon
salt and freshly ground pepper
¾ cup (6 fl oz/180 ml) heavy (double) cream, chilled
⅓ cup (3 fl oz/80 ml) brandy

Tarragon-flavored whipped cream gives this delicate soup a luxurious finish. For more depth of flavor, use a variety of mushrooms. Many so-called wild mushrooms—chanterelle, shiitake, oyster—are now cultivated and can be found in well-stocked food stores.

Brush the mushrooms clean. If using shiitakes, cut off the tough stems; trim the stem ends of the other mushrooms. Slice all of the mushrooms. Set aside.

In a large, heavy saucepan over medium heat, melt the butter. When hot, add the shallots and leeks and sauté, stirring occasionally, until golden brown, about 15 minutes. Add all the mushrooms and sauté, stirring frequently, until soft, about 5 minutes. Add the flour and cook, stirring constantly, for 3 minutes. Gradually pour in the beef stock or broth and chicken stock or broth, stirring until the liquid is smooth, and then add 1½ tablespoons of the tarragon. Raise the heat to high and bring to a boil, stirring constantly. Reduce the heat to medium-low and simmer, uncovered, for 20 minutes to blend the flavors. Season to taste with salt and pepper.

Meanwhile, in a bowl, using a whisk or an electric mixer set on high speed, beat the cream until soft peaks form. Using a rubber spatula, fold in the remaining 1 tablespoon tarragon. Season to taste with salt and pepper. Cover and refrigerate until serving.

Just before serving, mix the brandy into the soup. Ladle the soup into warmed bowls. Top each with a heaping tablespoon of the tarragon cream and serve.

Serves 8–10

Smoked Salmon Toasts

1½ tablespoons olive oil, plus oil for
 brushing toasts
1½ tablespoons fresh lime juice
8–10 slices country-style bread, each
 3 by 5 inches (7.5 by 13 cm) and
 ¼ inch (6 mm) thick
freshly ground pepper
1 lb (500 g) smoked salmon, thinly
 sliced
3 tablespoons chopped fresh tarragon
lime slices and lime zest strips,
 optional

Start off the celebration with these elegant toasts and a bottle of sparkling wine. For an equally tasty variation, replace the tarragon with arugula (rocket).

✿

*P*reheat an oven to 375°F (190°C).

In a small bowl, whisk together the 1½ tablespoons olive oil and the lime juice. Set aside.

Place the bread slices on a baking sheet. Bake until light brown, about 5 minutes. Turn over the slices and bake until light brown on the second side, about 5 minutes longer. Remove from the oven and brush with olive oil. Sprinkle with pepper.

Top the toasts with the salmon, dividing the slices evenly. Brush the salmon with the oil and lime juice mixture. Sprinkle with the tarragon. Cut each toast into 4 pieces and arrange on a platter. Garnish with lime slices and zest strips, if desired, and serve.

Serves 8–10

Butternut Squash Soup with Marsala and Thyme

1 butternut squash, about 3 lb (1.5 kg), halved lengthwise and fibers and seeds removed

6 slices bacon, chopped

2 large yellow onions, chopped

1½ tablespoons chopped fresh thyme or 1½ teaspoons dried thyme

5¼ cups (42 fl oz/1.3 l) chicken or vegetable stock or canned low-sodium broth, or as needed

⅓ cup (3 fl oz/80 ml) heavy (double) cream or half-and-half (half cream)

3 tablespoons dry Marsala or dry sherry

pinch of cayenne pepper

salt and freshly ground black pepper

fresh thyme leaves, optional

With its autumnal colors and flavors, this soup is an ideal first course for any fall meal. A dash of curry powder would make a lively variation. The soup can be prepared 1 day ahead and then reheated over medium heat just before serving.

Preheat an oven to 375°F (190°C).

In a baking pan, place the squash cut sides down. Add water to the pan to a depth of ¼ inch (6 mm). Bake until the squash is tender, about 50 minutes. Remove from the oven and let cool. Using a spoon, scrape the flesh from the skin. You will need 3¾ cups (30 oz/940 g) for this soup; reserve any remaining squash for another use.

In a large, heavy saucepan over medium heat, sauté the bacon until the fat is rendered, about 3 minutes. Add the onions and chopped or dried thyme and sauté until tender, about 8 minutes. Remove from the heat.

Transfer the onion mixture to a food processor fitted with the metal blade or to a blender. In 2 or more batches, add the squash and purée until smooth. Return the purée to the saucepan. Place over medium-low heat and mix in the 5¼ cups (42 fl oz/1.3 l) stock or broth. Simmer, uncovered, stirring occasionally, for 20 minutes to blend the flavors. Stir in the cream or half-and-half and the Marsala or sherry. Add the cayenne pepper and season to taste with salt and black pepper. If the soup is too thick, thin with additional stock to the desired consistency.

Ladle into individual bowls and garnish with thyme leaves, if desired. Serve hot.

Serves 8–10

Frisée, Pear and Prosciutto Salad

3 tablespoons cider vinegar

1 shallot, minced

1½ teaspoons Dijon mustard

1½ teaspoons honey

2 teaspoons chopped fresh thyme or
   ¾ teaspoon dried thyme

6 tablespoons (3 fl oz/90 ml) olive oil

2 firm but ripe pears such as Bosc or
   Anjou

10 cups (10 oz/315 g) frisée *(see note)*

3 oz (90 g) thinly sliced prosciutto, cut
   crosswise into strips ¼ inch (6 mm)
   wide

salt and freshly ground pepper

Luscious fall pears are the perfect counterpoint to crisp frisée and mildly salty prosciutto. A member of the chicory family, frisée has slightly bitter, curly leaves ranging from pale green to yellow-white. If frisée is unavailable, substitute chicory (curly endive). For easy serving, make the dressing early in the day. The pears can be sliced up to 30 minutes before serving, but you must mix them with 1 tablespoon of the dressing to prevent them from discoloring.

❧

*I*n a small bowl, whisk together the vinegar, shallot, mustard, honey and thyme. Gradually whisk in the olive oil until well blended.

Using a vegetable peeler, peel each pear. Cut into quarters through the stem end. Remove the core and slice the quarters lengthwise. Cut each slice in half crosswise.

In a large bowl, combine the pears, frisée and prosciutto. Drizzle on the dressing and toss to coat. Season to taste with salt and pepper and serve.

Serves 8–10

Rosemary and Spice Nuts

2½ cups (10 oz/315 g) mixed raw nuts
  (see note)
2 tablespoons olive oil
1½ tablespoons chopped fresh rosemary
1 tablespoon sugar
1½ teaspoons ground cumin
1 teaspoon salt
1 teaspoon freshly ground black pepper
¼ teaspoon cayenne pepper

The combination of fresh rosemary, cumin and cayenne pepper lends an irresistible depth of flavor to this nibble. The recipe calls for using mixed nuts; try pecans, walnuts and peanuts or your own favorites.

Preheat an oven to 300°F (150°C).

Place the nuts in a bowl. Pour the oil into a small, heavy saucepan and place over medium-low heat until warm. Add the rosemary and stir until the mixture is aromatic, about 1 minute. Pour the flavored oil over the nuts. Add the sugar, cumin, salt, black pepper and cayenne and stir to coat evenly. Transfer the nuts to a baking pan.

Bake, stirring occasionally, until the nuts are toasted, about 20 minutes. Remove from the oven and let cool completely. Store in an airtight container at room temperature for up to 4 days.

Makes about 2½ cups (10 oz/315 g)

Endive, Fennel and Walnut Salad

Offer this sophisticated first course before your favorite turkey or ham. Pecans or hazelnuts (filberts) can be used in place of the walnuts.

2 small fennel bulbs with stalks and feathery fronds attached

3 heads Belgian endive (chicory/witloof), cored and cut crosswise into 1-inch (2.5-cm) pieces

1 large head radicchio, cored and thinly sliced

½ cup (3 oz/90 g) slivered pitted Kalamata olives

2 tablespoons balsamic vinegar

1 tablespoon plus 1 teaspoon Dijon mustard

¼ cup (2 fl oz/60 ml) olive oil

salt and freshly ground pepper

¾ cup (3 oz/90 g) walnuts, toasted (*see glossary, page 106*) and coarsely chopped

8–10 tablespoons (2–2½ oz/60–75 g) coarsely grated Parmesan cheese

Cut off the stalks and feathery fronds from the fennel bulbs. Reserve the fronds and discard the stalks or reserve for another use. Remove any bruised outer leaves from each bulb and thinly slice the bulbs crosswise. Chop enough of the fronds to measure ¼ cup (⅓ oz/10 g).

In a large bowl, combine the sliced fennel, fennel fronds, endive, radicchio and olives. Toss to mix.

In a small bowl, whisk together the vinegar and mustard. Gradually whisk in the oil. Add to the salad and toss to coat. Season to taste with salt and pepper and mix in the walnuts.

Divide the salad evenly among individual plates. Sprinkle each serving with 1 tablespoon Parmesan cheese and serve.

Serves 8–10

Brandied Chestnut Soup

3 tablespoons butter
3 tablespoons olive oil
3 celery stalks with leaves, chopped
1 large yellow onion, chopped
2 bay leaves
⅓ cup (2 oz/60 g) all-purpose (plain)
   flour
3 qt (3 l) chicken stock or canned
   low-sodium broth
2¼ lb (1.1 kg) fresh chestnuts, boiled
   and peeled (*see glossary, page 104*) and
   halved
1½ cups (12 fl oz/375 ml) dry red wine
½–¾ teaspoon ground nutmeg
salt and freshly ground pepper

FOR THE CROUTONS:
2 tablespoons butter
3 cups (6 oz/185 g) cubed crustless
   white bread (½-inch/12-mm cubes)

⅓ cup (3 fl oz/80 ml) brandy

To save time, use 4½ cups (22 oz/690 g) vacuum-packed steamed chestnuts in place of the fresh chestnuts.

*I*n a large saucepan over medium heat, melt the butter with the oil. When hot, add the celery, onion and bay leaves and sauté, stirring occasionally, until the onion is tender, about 10 minutes. Add the flour and cook, stirring constantly, for 2 minutes. Gradually mix in the stock or broth, then add the chestnuts. Bring to a boil, reduce the heat to medium-low, cover partially and simmer until the chestnuts are very tender, about 45 minutes.

Remove the bay leaves and discard. Working in small batches, purée the soup in a blender. Return the purée to the saucepan and place over medium-high heat. Add the wine and ½ teaspoon nutmeg and bring to a boil. Season to taste with salt and pepper. Reduce the heat to low and keep hot.

To make the croutons, in a large, heavy frying pan over high heat, melt the butter. Add the bread cubes and sauté until golden brown on all sides, about 3 minutes.

Add the brandy to the soup. Taste and add the remaining ¼ teaspoon nutmeg if desired. Ladle into warmed bowls, top with the croutons and serve.

Serves 8–10

Shrimp and Grapefruit Cocktail

3–4 grapefruits

½ English (hothouse) cucumber

2 tablespoons tarragon vinegar

⅛ teaspoon salt

freshly ground pepper

1 teaspoon Dijon mustard

½ cup (4 fl oz/125 ml) extra-virgin olive oil

2 or 3 green (spring) onions, including tender green tops, minced (about 3 tablespoons)

1 tablespoon minced fresh tarragon, plus sprigs for garnish

1 tablespoon minced fresh parsley, preferably flat-leaf (Italian) parsley, plus sprigs for garnish

1½ lb (750 g) cooked and peeled bay shrimp

8–10 small butter (Boston) lettuce leaves

This recipe comes from Chuck Williams, who uses a tarragon-flavored sauce in place of the usual tomato cocktail sauce. If you cannot find already cooked and peeled bay shrimp, use 2 pounds (1 kg) small raw shrimp. Cook them in boiling salted water until pink and opaque throughout, 3–5 minutes; then drain, cool and peel.

Using a sharp knife, cut a thick slice from the bottom and top of each grapefruit to expose the flesh. Stand the fruit upright on a cutting board and thickly slice off the peel in wide strips, removing all the pith and membrane to expose the flesh. Working over a bowl, carefully cut along both sides of each segment to free it from the membrane, then cut in half crosswise and let the halves drop into the bowl. Cover and refrigerate. Peel the cucumber and cut lengthwise into quarters. If the seeds are large, cut away the seed section and discard. Slice each quarter crosswise into pieces ⅛ inch (3 mm) thick. Set aside.

In a small bowl, stir together the vinegar and salt until the salt dissolves. Stir in pepper to taste and the mustard. Gradually add the oil, whisking constantly until a slightly thickened dressing forms. Stir in the green onions and the minced tarragon and parsley. Taste and adjust the seasonings; set aside.

Discard any bits of shell from the shrimp and drain off any liquid. Place in a bowl, add the cucumber and the dressing and stir well. Cover and refrigerate for about 30 minutes; stir occasionally.

To serve, line footed compotes or small, shallow bowls with the lettuce leaves. Divide the grapefruit evenly among the leaves. Stir the shrimp mixture and spoon over the grapefruit, dividing it evenly. Spoon any excess dressing over the top. Garnish with the tarragon and parsley sprigs.

Serves 8–10

Herb-Rubbed Turkey with Mushroom Gravy

FOR THE TURKEY:
¼ cup (⅓ oz/10 g) chopped fresh parsley
3 tablespoons chopped fresh rosemary
3 tablespoons chopped fresh thyme
1 tablespoon freshly ground pepper
4 teaspoons salt
1 turkey, 14–16 lb (7–8 kg), neck and
  giblets reserved for making stock
fresh rosemary and thyme sprigs
2 tablespoons vegetable oil
¼ cup (2 oz/60 g) butter, melted

FOR THE GRAVY:
3¼ cups (26 fl oz/810 ml) turkey stock
  (*recipe on page 12*)
½ cup (4 oz/125 g) butter
6 large shallots, chopped
2 lb (1 kg) fresh cultivated white
  mushrooms, brushed clean and sliced
1 tablespoon chopped fresh thyme
⅓ cup (2 oz/60 g) all-purpose (plain)
  flour
1 cup (8 fl oz/250 ml) heavy (double)
  cream
salt and freshly ground pepper
1 cup (1½ oz/45 g) chopped fresh parsley

fresh rosemary and thyme sprigs

*P*osition a rack in the lower third of an oven and preheat to 325°F (165°C). To prepare the turkey, in a small bowl, stir together the chopped parsley, rosemary and thyme, and the pepper and salt. Rinse the turkey inside and out and dry with paper towels. Discard any pieces of fat from the cavities. Place the turkey on a rack in a large roasting pan. Slip the herb sprigs into the main cavity. Brush the outside of the bird with the oil and then rub the herb mixture all over the turkey. Tie the legs together. Tuck the wing tips under the body. Drizzle the butter evenly over the turkey.

Roast for 45 minutes, then baste with the pan juices. Continue roasting, basting every 20 minutes, until an instant-read thermometer inserted into the thickest part of the thigh away from the bone registers 180°F (82°C), about 2½ hours longer. Transfer to a platter, cover loosely with aluminum foil and let stand for 20 minutes. Pour the pan juices into a large measuring pitcher and skim off and discard the fat.

To make the gravy, pour the stock into the roasting pan and place on the stove top. Bring to a boil, scraping up any browned bits. Remove from the heat. In a large frying pan over medium-high heat, melt the butter. Add the shallots and stir to coat. Add the mushrooms and thyme and sauté until the mushrooms just start to soften, about 5 minutes. Add the flour and cook, stirring frequently, for 1 minute. Add the stock and the pan juices and bring to a boil, stirring constantly. Add the cream and boil, stirring occasionally, until the sauce thickens slightly, about 3 minutes. Season to taste with salt and pepper. Stir in the parsley.

Garnish the turkey with rosemary and thyme sprigs and carve at the table. Serve with the gravy.

Serves 8–10

Baked Ham with Apricot-Mustard Glaze

1 fully cooked, bone-in smoked whole
  ham, about 16 lb (8 kg)
about 40 whole cloves
1 cup (8 fl oz/250 ml) apricot nectar
1 cup (8 fl oz/250 ml) water
2 tablespoons chopped fresh thyme or
  2 teaspoons dried thyme
½ cup (5 oz/155 g) apricot preserves
½ cup (4 fl oz/125 ml) bourbon
¼ cup (2 oz/60 g) Dijon mustard
⅓ cup (2½ oz/75 g) firmly packed
  golden brown sugar

A succulent ham, a traditional alternative to turkey, is easier to prepare than a turkey and every bit as delicious.

Position a rack in the lower third of an oven and preheat to 425°F (220°C). Line a large roasting pan with aluminum foil.

Place the ham fat side up in the prepared pan. Trim off any rind and fat, leaving a fat layer ¼ inch (6 mm) thick. Cut parallel diagonal lines ¼ inch (6 mm) deep in the fat and 1 inch (2.5 cm) apart. Cut in the same manner in the opposite direction, to create a diamond pattern. Press the cloves into the intersections of the lines or the centers of the diamonds. Pour the apricot nectar and the water over the ham. Sprinkle with the thyme.

Bake the ham, basting every 15 minutes with the pan juices, for 3 minutes per pound; a 16-lb (8 kg) ham would be heated through in about 48 minutes.

Meanwhile, in a small, heavy saucepan, combine the apricot preserves, bourbon and mustard and whisk until smooth. Place over medium heat and stir until the preserves melt, forming a glaze. Remove from the heat and set aside.

Remove the ham from the oven and increase the oven temperature to 450°F (230°C). Brush all of the glaze generously over the ham. Sprinkle the brown sugar evenly over the glaze. Return the ham to the oven and bake until deep brown, about 30 minutes. Transfer to a large serving platter, cover loosely with aluminum foil and let stand for about 20 minutes before carving.

Serves 16

Cider-Glazed Turkey with Cider-Shallot Gravy

FOR THE TURKEY:

3 cups (24 fl oz/750 ml) apple cider or
  apple juice
¾ cup (6 oz/185 g) butter, at room
  temperature
2 tablespoons chopped fresh thyme or
  2 teaspoons dried thyme
1 turkey, 14–16 lb (7–8 kg), neck and
  giblets reserved for making stock
salt and freshly ground pepper

FOR THE GRAVY:

6 tablespoons (3 oz/90 g) butter
3 oz (90 g) shallots, sliced
2 tablespoons chopped fresh thyme or
  2 teaspoons dried thyme
6 tablespoons (2 oz/60 g) all-purpose
  (plain) flour
about 4½ cups (36 fl oz/1.1 l) turkey
  stock (*recipe on page 12*)
3 tablespoons Calvados, applejack or
  brandy
salt and freshly ground pepper

fresh thyme sprigs, optional

To prepare the turkey, in a saucepan over high heat, bring the cider or juice to a boil; boil until reduced to 1 cup (8 fl oz/250 ml), about 30 minutes. Set aside ½ cup (4 fl oz/125 ml). Mix the butter and thyme into the remaining ½ cup (4 fl oz/125 ml) cider or juice; refrigerate until cold. Position a rack in the lower third of an oven and preheat to 325°F (165°C). Rinse the turkey inside and out and dry with paper towels. Discard any pieces of fat from the cavities. Place the turkey on a rack in a large roasting pan. Spread the cider butter inside and over the outside of the turkey. Sprinkle with salt and pepper. Tie the legs together. Tuck the wing tips under the body.

Roast for 45 minutes, then baste with the pan juices. Continue roasting, basting every 20 minutes and covering with aluminum foil when dark brown, until an instant-read thermometer inserted into the thickest part of the thigh away from the bone registers 180°F (82°C), about 2½ hours longer. Transfer to a platter, cover loosely with foil and let stand for 20 minutes. Pour the pan juices into a large measuring pitcher; skim off and discard the fat.

To make the gravy, in a saucepan over medium-high heat, melt the butter. Add the shallots and thyme and sauté until the shallots are golden brown, about 8 minutes. Add the flour and cook, stirring frequently, until browned, about 5 minutes. Add enough stock to the pan juices to measure 5 cups (40 fl oz/1.25 l). Gradually whisk the stock mixture into the butter mixture. Bring to a boil, whisking frequently. Mix in the reduced cider or juice and boil until thickened, about 10 minutes. Mix in the Calvados or other brandy and return to a boil. Season with salt and pepper.

Garnish the turkey with thyme sprigs, if desired, and carve at the table. Serve with the gravy.

Serves 8–10

Roasted Fall Vegetables with Wild Rice Pilaf

2 tan-skinned sweet potatoes, well
   scrubbed
4 parsnips, peeled
2 small acorn squashes
2 large red bell peppers (capsicums)
1 lb (500 g) white boiling onions,
   1–1½ inches (2.5–4 cm) in diameter,
   unpeeled
8 shallots, peeled and halved
4 tablespoons (2 fl oz/60 ml) olive oil
6 tablespoons (3 oz/90 g) butter
2 teaspoons ground cinnamon
2 teaspoons ground turmeric
salt and freshly ground pepper
4 bay leaves
wild rice and dried cranberry pilaf
   (recipe on page 48)

A cornucopia of autumn's offerings surrounds a pilaf accented with holiday spices to create a spectacular meatless Thanksgiving main course. It can also round out a meal featuring turkey or ham.

Preheat an oven to 425°F (220°C).

Halve the sweet potatoes crosswise, then cut each half lengthwise into 8 wedges. Cut the parsnips in half crosswise, then cut in half lengthwise. Cut the acorn squashes in half crosswise and remove and discard the seeds and any fibers. Cut each half lengthwise into 8 wedges, then cut each wedge in half crosswise. Trim off the peel from the squash pieces. Cut each bell pepper lengthwise into quarters. Remove and discard the seeds and ribs and cut each quarter in half crosswise.

Bring a large pot three-fourths full of water to a boil. Add the onions and boil for 3 minutes to loosen the skins. Drain and rinse with cold water to cool; drain again. Cut off the root and stem ends from each onion and slip off the skins.

Divide the sweet potatoes, parsnips, squashes, bell peppers, onions and shallots between 2 large baking pans. Drizzle 2 tablespoons of the oil and dot 3 tablespoons of the butter evenly over the contents of each pan. Sprinkle each with 1 teaspoon cinnamon and 1 teaspoon turmeric. Sprinkle with salt and pepper. Add 2 bay leaves to each pan. Stir to coat the vegetables.

Roast, stirring occasionally, until the vegetables are golden brown and tender when pierced with a fork, about 1 hour.

Meanwhile, make the pilaf and mound in the center of a large platter. Surround with the vegetables and serve.

Serves 8

Roast Turkey Breast with Rosemary-Mustard Butter

FOR THE TURKEY BREAST:

1 whole turkey breast with bone,
  4 lb (2 kg)
¼ cup (2 oz/60 g) butter, at room
  temperature
1½ tablespoons chopped fresh rosemary
  or 1½ teaspoons dried rosemary
1 tablespoon Dijon mustard
salt and freshly ground pepper

FOR THE GRAVY:

½ cup (4 fl oz/125 ml) dry vermouth
3 tablespoons butter
2 shallots, chopped
1½ teaspoons chopped fresh rosemary
  or ½ teaspoon dried rosemary
3 tablespoons all-purpose (plain) flour
2 cups (16 fl oz/500 ml) turkey stock
  (recipe on page 12)
salt and freshly ground pepper

fresh rosemary sprigs, optional

A bone-in turkey breast is the perfect star of the Thanksgiving table for a small group.

Preheat an oven to 350°F (180°C). To prepare the turkey breast, rinse and dry with paper towels. Place on a rack in a large roasting pan. In a small bowl, mix together the butter, rosemary and mustard. Spread evenly over the entire turkey breast. Sprinkle with salt and pepper. Roast, basting every 20 minutes with the pan drippings, until an instant-read thermometer inserted into the thickest part of the breast away from the bone registers 170°F (77°C), about 1¾ hours. Transfer to a platter, cover loosely with aluminum foil and let stand for 20 minutes.

To make the gravy, pour off the drippings from the roasting pan and discard. Add the vermouth to the pan and place on the stove top over medium-high heat. Bring to a boil, scraping up any browned bits. Boil until reduced to 1 tablespoon, about 2 minutes. Remove from the heat. In a saucepan over medium heat, melt the butter. Add the shallots and rosemary and sauté until the shallots are tender, about 3 minutes. Add the flour and cook, stirring frequently, until golden brown, about 4 minutes. Gradually whisk in the stock and the reduced vermouth. Bring to a boil, stirring constantly. Boil, stirring occasionally, until reduced to a sauce consistency, about 5 minutes. Season to taste with salt and pepper.

Garnish the turkey breast with the rosemary sprigs, if desired, and carve at the table. Serve with the gravy.

Serves 4–6

Maple-Glazed Turkey with Gingersnap Gravy

FOR THE TURKEY:
1 turkey, 14–16 lb (7–8 kg), neck and
    giblets reserved for making stock
¼ cup (2 oz/60 g) butter, melted
1 tablespoon chopped fresh sage or
    1 teaspoon dried sage
1 tablespoon chopped fresh thyme or
    1 teaspoon dried thyme
salt and freshly ground pepper
2 cups (16 fl oz/500 ml) chicken stock
    or canned low-sodium broth
1 tablespoon pure maple syrup

FOR THE GRAVY:
3 tablespoons butter
5 shallots, chopped
1½ tablespoons chopped fresh sage or
    ¾ teaspoon dried sage
1½ tablespoons chopped fresh thyme or
    ¾ teaspoon dried thyme
¾ teaspoon ground ginger
4½ cups (36 fl oz/1.1 l) turkey stock
    (recipe on page 12)
9 gingersnap cookies, crumbled
salt and freshly ground pepper

fresh sage and thyme sprigs, optional

Position a rack in the lower third of an oven and preheat to 325°F (165°C).

To prepare the turkey, rinse inside and out and dry with paper towels. Discard any pieces of fat from the cavities. Place the turkey on a rack in a large roasting pan. Brush with half of the melted butter. Sprinkle with the sage and thyme and season with salt and pepper. Tie the legs together. Tuck the wing tips under the body. Pour the stock or broth into the roasting pan.

Roast the turkey, basting with the pan juices every 30 minutes, for 2¾ hours. Mix the maple syrup into the remaining melted butter. Brush the glaze over the turkey. Continue to roast until an instant-read thermometer inserted into the thickest part of the thigh away from the bone registers 180°F (82°C), about 30 minutes longer. Transfer to a platter, cover loosely with aluminum foil and let stand for 20 minutes. Pour the pan juices into a large measuring pitcher and skim off and discard the fat.

To make the gravy, in a large saucepan over medium heat, melt the butter. Add the shallots and sauté until tender, about 3 minutes. Add the sage, thyme and ginger and stir for 1 minute to blend the flavors. Add the stock and bring to a boil. Boil until reduced to 3 cups (24 fl oz/750 ml), about 20 minutes. Add the pan juices and the gingersnaps and boil, whisking frequently, until thickened to a thin gravy, about 10 minutes. Season to taste with salt and pepper.

Garnish the turkey with sage and thyme sprigs, if desired, and carve at the table. Serve with the gravy.

Serves 8–10

Sweet Potatoes with Brown Butter and Parmesan Cheese

4 lb (2 kg) tan-skinned sweet potatoes, peeled and cut into 1-inch (2.5 cm) cubes

½ cup (4 oz/125 g) plus 2 tablespoons unsalted butter

¼ cup (⅓ oz/10 g) chopped fresh sage or 1½ tablespoons dried sage

salt and freshly ground pepper

1¼ cups (5 oz/150 g) freshly grated Parmesan cheese

fresh sage sprigs, optional

Here is a dish for people who do not like their sweet potatoes sweet. The chestnut-flavored, tan-skinned sweet potatoes are best for this recipe, or acorn squash can be used in their place. Ready the dish in the morning, then bake in the oven while the turkey or ham rests.

🦃

*P*lace the potatoes on a steamer rack and set over a steamer pan of boiling water. Do not allow the rack to touch the water. Cover and steam until just tender when pierced with a fork, about 15 minutes. Remove from the steamer and let cool.

Preheat an oven to 400°F (200°C). Butter a 13-by-9-by-2-inch (33-by-23-by-5-cm) baking dish. Transfer the sweet potatoes to the dish.

In a heavy frying pan over medium-low heat, melt the butter and cook, swirling the pan occasionally, until the butter is golden brown, about 5 minutes. Add the chopped or dried sage and salt and pepper to taste. Continue to cook until the butter is a deep golden brown, about 2 minutes longer. Pour the browned butter over the sweet potatoes. Sprinkle evenly with ¾ cup (3 oz/90 g) of the cheese. Stir to coat. Taste and add more salt and pepper, if desired. Cover the dish with aluminum foil.

Bake the sweet potatoes until heated through, about 20 minutes. Transfer to a warmed serving platter and sprinkle evenly with the remaining ½ cup (2 oz/60 g) Parmesan. Garnish with sage sprigs, if desired, and serve at once.

Serves 8–10

Wild Rice and Dried Cranberry Pilaf

9 cups (72 fl oz/2.25 l) low-sodium
 vegetable broth or 4½ cups (36 fl oz/
 1.1 l) each broth and water
1⅓ cups (8 oz/250 g) wild rice, well
 rinsed
¼ cup (2 oz/60 g) butter
3 large yellow onions, chopped
¾ teaspoon ground cardamom
1 teaspoon ground allspice
2 bay leaves
1 cup (4 oz/125 g) dried cranberries
1 cup (6 oz/185 g) golden raisins
 (sultanas)
2 teaspoons grated orange zest
salt and freshly ground pepper
1½ cups (10½ oz/330 g) long-grain
 white rice
½ cup (2½ oz/75 g) pine nuts, toasted
 (*see glossary, page 106*)
½ cup (¾ oz/20 g) chopped fresh parsley,
 plus sprigs for garnish, optional
orange zest strips, optional

This dish combining pine nuts, dried cranberries and raisins with wild and long-grain rice makes a delicious addition to a Thanksgiving dinner featuring turkey or ham. It also complements the vegetarian main course of roasted fall vegetables (recipe on page 40).

*I*n a saucepan over high heat, bring 6 cups (48 fl oz/1.5 l) vegetable stock or 3 cups (24 fl oz/750 ml) each broth and water to a boil. Add the wild rice and return to a boil. Reduce the heat to medium and simmer uncovered, stirring occasionally, until the rice is tender but still slightly firm to the bite, about 40 minutes.

Meanwhile, in a large, heavy saucepan over medium-high heat, melt the butter. When hot, add the onions and sauté, stirring occasionally, until tender, about 12 minutes. Add the cardamom and allspice and stir for about 20 seconds until aromatic. Add the remaining 3 cups (24 fl oz/750 ml) stock or 1½ cups (12 fl oz/375 ml) each broth and water, bay leaves, dried cranberries, raisins and grated orange zest. Season to taste with salt and pepper. Bring to a boil. Add the white rice, reduce the heat to low, cover and cook until the liquid is absorbed and the rice is tender, about 20 minutes.

Drain the wild rice well. Remove the bay leaves from the white rice mixture and discard. Gently mix the wild rice into the white rice. Stir in the pine nuts and chopped parsley. Taste and adjust the seasonings. Transfer to a warmed serving bowl. Garnish with parsley sprigs and zest strips, if desired, and serve at once.

Serves 8–10

Spoonbread

4½ cups (36 fl oz/1.1 l) milk
1½ cups (7½ oz/235 g) yellow cornmeal
1½ teaspoons salt
⅛ teaspoon freshly grated nutmeg
3 tablespoons unsalted butter, cut into
small cubes
6 eggs, separated
2 teaspoons baking powder
½ cup (2 oz/60 g) freshly grated
Parmesan cheese

This recipe from Chuck Williams for spoonbread, a tradition in the southern United States, has the characteristics of a soufflé because the egg whites are beaten separately and then folded into the cornmeal mixture. When served, it can be topped with a tomato sauce.

Preheat an oven to 400°F (200°C). Butter a 3-qt (3-l) baking dish with sides 2–2½ inches (5–6 mm) deep.

Pour 4 cups (32 fl oz/1 l) of the milk into a saucepan, place over medium heat and heat until small bubbles appear along the edges of the pan. Remove from the heat and, using a whisk, stir vigorously while slowly pouring in the cornmeal. Continue to whisk until the mixture is smooth. Return to medium heat and stir until thickened, 1–2 minutes.

Remove from the heat and stir in the remaining ½ cup (4 fl oz/125 ml) milk and the salt, nutmeg and butter, stirring continuously until the butter melts. Add the egg yolks one at a time, stirring well after each addition. Stir in the baking powder and Parmesan cheese.

In a bowl, using a whisk or an electric mixer set on medium speed, beat the egg whites until soft peaks form. Using a rubber spatula, stir about one-fourth of the beaten egg whites into the cornmeal mixture to lighten it, then carefully fold in the remaining whites just until no whites remain. Immediately spoon the batter into the prepared baking dish.

Bake until puffed and golden and a toothpick inserted into the center comes out clean, 45–50 minutes. Remove from the oven and serve at once.

Serves 10–12

Creamed Turnips and Chard

2 lb (1 kg) turnips, peeled and cut into
   ¾-inch (2-cm) pieces

8 slices bacon, finely chopped

5 tablespoons (2 oz/60 g) all-purpose
   (plain) flour

2¾ cups (22 fl oz/680 ml) milk

½ cup (4 fl oz/125 ml) half-and-half
   (half cream)

½ teaspoon ground nutmeg

1 large bunch green Swiss chard, about
   1 lb (500 g), stems removed and
   leaves thinly sliced crosswise

salt and freshly ground pepper

The creamy sauce that envelops the turnips and chard makes for a particularly luscious and homey side dish that complements turkey as well as other vegetables, such as sweet potatoes with brown butter and Parmesan cheese (recipe on page 47). Replace the bacon with ¼ cup (2 oz/60 g) butter if you prefer. This dish can be prepared 1 day ahead and then reheated over medium-low heat shortly before serving.

*F*ill a large pot three-fourths full with water, salt it lightly and bring to a boil over high heat. Add the turnips and boil until just tender when pierced with a fork, about 5 minutes. Drain well and set aside.

In a heavy saucepan over medium heat, cook the bacon, stirring frequently, until the fat is rendered and the bacon begins to brown, about 5 minutes. Add the flour and cook, stirring frequently, for 2 minutes. Gradually whisk in the milk. Bring to a simmer, stirring constantly. Reduce the heat to low and simmer, uncovered, until thickened to a medium-thick cream sauce, about 5 minutes.

Gradually stir in the half-and-half and nutmeg. Add the chard leaves and simmer over medium-low heat, stirring frequently, until just tender, about 4 minutes. Add the turnips and stir until heated through, about 3 minutes.

Season to taste with salt and pepper. Transfer to a warmed serving dish and serve at once.

Serves 8–10

Caramelized Onion and Mushroom Stuffing

1 lb (500 g) buttermilk bread or egg
  bread, cut into ½-inch (12-mm) cubes
6 tablespoons (3 oz/90 g) butter
2 large yellow onions, chopped
1 lb (500 g) fresh cultivated white
  mushrooms, brushed clean and sliced
3 celery stalks, chopped
2 tablespoons chopped fresh tarragon or
  2 teaspoons dried tarragon
½ cup (¾ oz/20 g) chopped fresh
  parsley
¾ cup (6 fl oz/180 ml) chicken stock or
  canned low-sodium broth
salt and freshly ground pepper
2 eggs, beaten until blended

Preheat an oven to 400°F (200°C).

Spread the bread cubes in a single layer in a large baking pan. Bake, stirring occasionally, until golden brown, about 10 minutes. Transfer to a large bowl.

In a large, heavy frying pan over medium-high heat, melt the butter. When hot, add the onions and cook, stirring occasionally, until golden brown, about 20 minutes. Reduce the heat to medium. Add the mushrooms and celery and cook, stirring frequently, until tender, about 8 minutes. Add to the bread cubes, along with the tarragon and parsley. Add the stock or broth to the same pan and bring to a boil, scraping up any browned bits. Add to the bread and season to taste with salt and pepper. Mix in the eggs.

To bake the stuffing in a turkey: Fill the cavities with the stuffing and truss as directed on page 9; increase the roasting time of the turkey by 30 minutes. Butter a baking dish large enough to hold the remaining stuffing and spoon the stuffing into it; cover with aluminum foil. Bake alongside the turkey for 30 minutes. Uncover and bake until the top is golden brown, about 30 minutes longer.

To bake all the stuffing in a baking dish: Preheat an oven to 325°F (165°C). Butter a 13-by-9-by-2-inch (33-by-23-by-5-cm) baking dish and spoon the stuffing into it. Cover with foil and bake for 30 minutes. Uncover and bake until the top is golden brown, about 30 minutes longer.

Makes about 12 cups (4½ lb/2.25 kg) stuffing, enough for a 16 lb (8 kg) turkey; serves 8–10

Mashed Potatoes with Basil and Chives

5 lb (2.5 kg) baking potatoes, peeled and cut into 2-inch (5-cm) pieces

5 tablespoons (2½ oz/75 g) butter, at room temperature

1–1¼ cups (8–10 fl oz/250–310 ml) milk, warmed

½ cup (¾ oz/20 g) packed chopped fresh basil, plus sprigs for garnish

⅓ cup (½ oz/15 g) chopped fresh chives, plus chives for garnish

salt and freshly ground pepper

Updated with a generous amount of chopped fresh herbs, this holiday standard is terrific with roast chicken or roast beef as well as turkey. The mashed potatoes can be made 2 hours ahead and, just before serving, reheated over medium heat, stirring frequently with a wooden spoon and thinning with more milk if necessary.

*F*ill a large pot three-fourths full with water, salt it lightly and bring to a boil over high heat. Add the potatoes and boil until tender when pierced with a fork, about 20 minutes. Drain well.

Immediately transfer the potatoes to a large bowl. Add the butter. Using an electric mixer set on medium speed, a potato masher or a wooden spoon, beat until almost smooth. Add the 1 cup (8 fl oz/250 ml) milk, chopped basil and ⅓ cup (½ oz/15 g) chopped chives and mash with the masher or wooden spoon until smooth. Add more milk as needed to achieve a creamy texture. Season to taste with salt and pepper.

Transfer to a warmed bowl and garnish with basil sprigs and chives. Serve hot.

Serves 8–10

Herbed Corn Bread and Red Pepper Stuffing

herbed corn bread (recipe on page 87),
  cut into ½-inch (12-mm) cubes
¼ cup (2 oz/60 g) butter
2 large red bell peppers (capsicums),
  seeded, deribbed and chopped
2 large yellow onions, chopped
3 celery stalks, chopped
2 teaspoons dried sage
2 teaspoons dried marjoram
1 tablespoon chili powder
salt and freshly ground pepper
4 eggs, beaten until blended
1½ cups (12 fl oz/375 ml) chicken
  stock or canned low-sodium broth

Preheat an oven to 375°F (190°C). Spread the corn bread cubes in a large jelly-roll pan. Bake, stirring occasionally, until slightly dry and toasted, about 30 minutes. Transfer the cubes to a large bowl.

In a large, heavy frying pan over high heat, melt the butter. When hot, add the bell peppers, onions, celery, sage and marjoram and sauté, stirring frequently, until the vegetables are tender, about 20 minutes. Add to the bread cubes. Mix in the chili powder. Season to taste with salt and pepper. Mix in the eggs.

To bake the stuffing in a turkey: Stir ½ cup (4 fl oz/125 ml) of the stock or broth into the stuffing. Fill the cavities with the stuffing and truss as directed on page 9; increase the roasting time of the turkey by 30 minutes. Mix enough of the remaining chicken stock into the remaining stuffing to moisten slightly (½–1 cup/4–8 fl oz/125–250 ml, depending on the amount of remaining stuffing). Butter a baking dish large enough to hold the stuffing and spoon the stuffing into it; cover with aluminum foil. Bake alongside the turkey for 30 minutes. Uncover and bake until the top begins to brown, about 15 minutes longer.

To bake all the stuffing in a baking dish: Preheat an oven to 325°F (165°C). Butter a 13-by-9-by-2-inch (33-by-23-by-5-cm) baking dish. Mix 1½ cups (12 fl oz/375 ml) stock or broth into the stuffing. Transfer to the prepared dish. Cover with foil. Bake until the stuffing is firm and heated through, about 45 minutes. Uncover and bake until the top begins to brown, about 15 minutes longer.

Makes about 12 cups (4½ lb/2.25 kg) stuffing, enough for a 16 lb (8 kg) turkey; serves 8–10

Sautéed Carrots, Parsnips and Onions

¼ cup (2 fl oz/60 ml) olive oil
1 yellow onion, chopped
2 tablespoons chopped fresh rosemary
   or 2 teaspoons dried rosemary
6 large carrots, peeled and sliced on
   the diagonal ¼ inch (6 mm) thick
6 parsnips, peeled and sliced on the
   diagonal ¼ inch (6 mm) thick
salt and freshly ground pepper

Tender-crisp fall vegetables make a savory side dish for a roasted turkey. Use a very large, heavy frying pan or a heavy pot for this quick sauté. Substitute 1½ cups (6 oz/185 g) sliced shallots or 1½ cups (4½ oz/140 g) sliced leeks for the onion for a satisfying variation.

*I*n a large, heavy frying pan or pot over medium heat, warm the oil. When hot, add the onion and rosemary and sauté, stirring frequently, until the onion begins to soften, about 5 minutes. Add the carrots and parsnips and sauté, stirring occasionally, until tender-crisp and starting to brown, about 15 minutes. Season to taste with salt and pepper.

Transfer to a warmed serving dish and serve at once.

Serves 8–10

Green Beans with Ham and Shallots

3 lb (1.5 kg) green beans, stem ends
 trimmed
6 tablespoons (3 oz/90 g) butter
6 oz (185 g) shallots, sliced
¼ lb (125 g) cooked ham, cut into
 slivers
salt and freshly ground pepper

Browned shallots and piquant ham add just the right touch to this seasonal side dish. To make preparations easier at mealtime, boil the beans the day before, cool completely and drain well, then wrap in plastic and refrigerate. Sauté the shallots and add the beans and ham just before serving.

*F*ill a large pot three-fourths full with water, salt it lightly and bring to a boil over high heat. Add the green beans and cook until just tender-crisp, about 5 minutes. Drain and rinse with cold water to cool; drain again.

In a large, heavy frying pan over medium-high heat, melt 4 tablespoons (2 oz/60 g) of the butter. When hot, add the shallots and sauté, stirring frequently, until they begin to brown, about 5 minutes. Add the remaining 2 tablespoons butter, the beans and the ham and toss until heated through, about 5 minutes.

Season to taste with salt and pepper. Transfer to a warmed platter and serve at once.

Serves 8–10

Mashed Yams with Brown Sugar and Spice

6 lb (3 kg) yams (*see note*)

1 cup (7 oz/210 g) firmly packed brown sugar

½ cup (4 fl oz/125 ml) heavy (double) cream or half-and-half (half cream)

6 tablespoons (3 oz/90 g) butter, at room temperature

1 teaspoon ground cinnamon

½ teaspoon ground nutmeg

½ teaspoon ground allspice

1 tablespoon vanilla extract (essence)

salt

½ cup (2 oz/60 g) coarsely chopped pecans

Assemble this festive dish the day before the feast and cover and store in the refrigerator, then bring to room temperature and slip into the oven about 30 minutes before serving. For the best flavor, use the red-skinned sweet potatoes marketed as yams. They are sweeter and more tender than the tan-skinned variety.

Preheat an oven to 325°F (165°C).

Place the yams on a baking sheet. Pierce in several places with a fork. Bake until very tender when pierced with a fork, about 1 hour. Remove from the oven and let cool slightly. Maintain the oven temperature.

Butter a 2- to 3-qt (2- to 3-l) baking dish. Halve the yams and, using a spoon, scrape the flesh from the skins into a large bowl. Add ¾ cup (6 oz/180 g) of the brown sugar and the cream or half-and-half, butter, cinnamon, nutmeg, allspice and vanilla. Using an electric mixer set on medium speed, a potato masher or a wooden spoon, beat until smooth, about 2 minutes. Season to taste with salt. Spoon into the prepared baking dish, smoothing the top. Sprinkle the pecans and the remaining ¼ cup (1 oz/30 g) sugar evenly over the top.

Bake until heated through, about 30 minutes. Serve hot directly from the dish.

Serves 8–10

Minted Boiling Onions

3 lb (1.5 kg) white boiling onions,
   about 1½ inches (4 cm) in diameter,
   unpeeled
¼ cup (2 oz/60 g) butter
1 cup (8 fl oz/125 ml) dry sherry
½ cup (4 fl oz/125 ml) beef stock or
   canned low-sodium broth
2 teaspoons honey
salt and freshly ground pepper
¼ cup (⅓ oz/10 g) chopped fresh mint,
   plus sprigs for garnish

*These onions can be simmered in the liquid early in the day.
Just before serving, boil to reduce the liquid to a glaze and add
the mint. Replacing the mint with 2 tablespoons chopped fresh
rosemary or thyme makes a delicious variation.*

Bring a large pot three-fourths full of water to a boil over
high heat. Add the onions and boil for 3 minutes to loosen
the skins. Drain and rinse with cold water to cool; drain
again. Cut off the root and stem ends from each onion and
slip off the skins.

In a large, heavy frying pan over medium-high heat,
melt the butter. When hot, add the onions, sherry, stock
or broth and honey. Season to taste with salt and pepper
and bring to a boil. Reduce the heat to very low, cover and
simmer gently, stirring occasionally, until the onions are
tender, about 45 minutes.

Uncover the frying pan, raise the heat to high and boil until
the liquid evaporates and the onions are glazed, about 5
minutes. Sprinkle with the chopped mint. Taste and adjust
the seasonings. Transfer to a warmed serving dish, garnish
with mint sprigs and serve at once.

Serves 8–10

Sautéed Corn with Chipotle Chilies and Thyme

½ cup (4 oz/125 g) butter
3 shallots, chopped
1 tablespoon finely chopped canned
  chipotle chilies (*see note*)
3 packages (1 lb/500 g each) frozen
  petite white corn kernels, thawed and
  well drained (*see note*)
2 tablespoons chopped fresh thyme
  or 2 teaspoons dried thyme
salt and freshly ground pepper
fresh thyme sprigs, optional

This flavorful sauté takes only minutes to prepare. Chipotle chilies are ripe jalapeño chilies that have been smoked. They are canned in a sauce, en adobo, *which consists of tomatoes, vinegar, onions and herbs, and lend a spicy, smoky nuance to the corn. Petite white corn kernels can be found in the frozen vegetable section of well-stocked food stores.*

In a large, heavy frying pan over medium heat, melt the butter. When hot, add the shallots and sauté, stirring, until tender, about 2 minutes. Add the chilies and stir for 30 seconds longer.

   Add the corn and chopped or dried thyme and cook, stirring frequently, until tender, about 5 minutes. Season to taste with salt and pepper and transfer to a warmed serving dish. Garnish with thyme sprigs, if desired, and serve at once.

Serves 8–10

Dried Fruit, Nut and Apple Stuffing

1 loaf sliced whole-wheat (wholemeal) bread, 1 lb (500 g), cut into ½-inch (12-mm) cubes

1 cup (6 oz/185 g) chopped dried figs

1 cup (4 oz/125 g) dried cranberries

½ cup (3 oz/90 g) golden raisins (sultanas)

½ cup (3 oz/90 g) chopped pitted prunes

1 cup (4 oz/125 g) walnuts, toasted (*see glossary, page 106*) and coarsely chopped

1 cup (5½ oz/170 g) whole almonds, toasted (*see glossary, page 106*) and coarsely chopped

¼ cup (2 oz/60 g) butter

2 large yellow onions, chopped

2 tart green apples such as pippin or Granny Smith, quartered, cored and chopped

3 celery stalks with leaves, chopped

½ cup (¾ oz/20 g) chopped fresh parsley

1½ tablespoons dried marjoram

¾ cup (6 fl oz/180 ml) chicken stock or canned low-sodium broth

salt and freshly ground pepper

2 eggs, beaten until blended

*P*reheat an oven to 400°F (200°C).

Place the bread cubes in a single layer in a large baking pan. Bake, stirring occasionally, until golden brown, about 10 minutes. Remove from the oven and transfer to a large bowl. Let cool, then crumble slightly with your fingers. Add the figs, dried cranberries, raisins, prunes, walnuts and almonds.

In a large, heavy frying pan over medium heat, melt the butter. When hot, add the onions, apples and celery and sauté, stirring frequently, until the onions and celery are tender, about 15 minutes. Add to the bread mixture. Mix in the parsley and marjoram. Add the stock or broth to the same frying pan and place over high heat. Bring to a boil, scraping up any browned bits. Add to the bread mixture and mix well. Season to taste with salt and pepper. Mix in the eggs.

To bake the stuffing in a turkey: Fill the cavities with the stuffing and truss as directed on page 9; increase the roasting time of the turkey by 30 minutes. Butter a baking dish large enough to hold the remaining stuffing and spoon the stuffing into it; cover with aluminum foil. Bake alongside the turkey for 45 minutes. Uncover and bake until the top is brown, about 15 minutes longer.

To bake all the stuffing in a baking dish: Preheat an oven to 325°F (165°C). Butter a 13-by-9-by-2-inch (33-by-23-by-5-cm) baking dish and spoon the stuffing into it. Cover with foil and bake for 45 minutes. Uncover and bake until the top is brown, about 15 minutes longer.

Makes about 12 cups (5 lb/2.5 kg) stuffing, enough for a 16 lb (8 kg) turkey; serves 8–10

Mashed Potatoes, Rutabagas and Sautéed Leeks

4 lb (2 kg) baking potatoes, peeled and
    cut into 2-inch (5-cm) pieces
2½ lb (1.25 kg) rutabagas (swedes),
    peeled, halved and thinly sliced
½ cup (4 oz/120 g) butter, at room
    temperature
4 leeks, white part and 1 inch (2.5 cm)
    of the green, halved lengthwise,
    carefully rinsed and thinly sliced
    crosswise
1 cup (8 fl oz/250 ml) milk, warmed
salt and freshly ground pepper
chopped fresh parsley

*Rutabagas add a pleasant nuttiness and sautéed leeks a touch
of oniony sweetness to mashed potatoes. If you like, make this
a few hours ahead, then reheat in a large saucepan over medium
heat, stirring frequently with a wooden spoon and thinning with
milk if necessary.*

*F*ill a large pot three-fourths full with water, salt it lightly
and bring to a boil over high heat. Add the potatoes and
rutabagas and boil until tender when pierced with a fork,
about 20 minutes.

Meanwhile, in a large, heavy frying pan over medium-
high heat, melt ¼ cup (2 oz/60 g) of the butter. When hot,
add the leeks and sauté, stirring, until tender and beginning
to brown, about 8 minutes. Remove from the heat and
keep warm.

Drain the potatoes and rutabagas well and immediately
transfer to a large bowl. Using an electric mixer set on
medium speed, a potato masher or a wooden spoon, beat
until smooth. Add the milk and again beat until smooth.
Mix in the remaining ¼ cup (2 oz/60 g) butter and the
leeks. Season to taste with salt and pepper.

Transfer to a warmed serving bowl, sprinkle with the
parsley and serve hot.

Serves 8–10

Brussels Sprouts with Orange Butter and Hazelnuts

2½ lb (1.25 kg) Brussels sprouts, trimmed and halved through the stem end
6 tablespoons (3 oz/90 g) butter
4 teaspoons grated orange zest
salt and freshly ground pepper
½ cup (2½ oz/75 g) hazelnuts (filberts), toasted and skinned (*see glossary, page 106*) and coarsely chopped

Grated orange zest lends a lively touch and hazelnuts add a wonderful crunch to this traditional holiday vegetable. Cutting the Brussels sprouts in half allows the densely layered leaves to absorb the flavorful zest-laced butter.

*F*ill a large pot three-fourths full with water, salt it lightly and bring to a boil over high heat. Add the Brussels sprouts and boil until tender when pierced with a fork, about 8 minutes. Drain well.

In a large, heavy saucepan over medium heat, melt the butter. Add the orange zest and Brussels sprouts and stir until the Brussels sprouts are heated through, about 5 minutes. Season to taste with salt and pepper.

Transfer to a large warmed bowl. Sprinkle with the hazelnuts and serve at once.

Serves 8–10

Sausage, Apple and Chestnut Stuffing

1 lb (500 g) sourdough bread or country-style white bread, crusts trimmed, cut into ½-inch (12-mm) cubes

¾ lb (375 g) bulk pork sausage

¼ cup (2 oz/60 g) butter

1 large yellow onion, chopped

3 large celery stalks, chopped

2 large tart apples such as pippin or Granny Smith, peeled, quartered, cored and chopped

3 tablespoons chopped fresh thyme or 1 tablespoon dried thyme

¾ cup (6 fl oz/180 ml) chicken stock or canned low-sodium broth

1 lb (500 g) fresh chestnuts, baked and peeled (*see glossary, page 104*) and coarsely chopped

½ cup (¾ oz/20 g) chopped fresh parsley

salt and freshly ground pepper

2 eggs, beaten until blended

For the fresh chestnuts, you may substitute 2 cups (about 10 oz/315 g) vacuum-packed steamed chestnuts, which have already been peeled.

Preheat an oven to 400°F (200°C). Place the bread cubes in a large baking pan. Bake, stirring occasionally, until lightly golden, about 12 minutes. Transfer the bread to a large bowl. In a large frying pan over medium-high heat, cook the sausage, crumbling with a fork, until browned, about 10 minutes. Transfer to the bowl with the bread. Add the butter to the drippings in the pan, reduce the heat to medium and melt the butter. Add the onion and celery and sauté until tender, about 8 minutes. Add the apples and thyme and sauté for 1½ minutes. Add to the bread. Add the stock or broth to the pan and bring to a boil, scraping up any browned bits. Add to the bread. Mix in the chestnuts and parsley and season with salt and pepper. Mix in the eggs.

To bake the stuffing in a turkey: Fill the cavities with the stuffing and truss as directed on page 9; increase the roasting time of the turkey by 30 minutes. Butter a baking dish large enough to hold the remaining stuffing and spoon the stuffing into it; cover with aluminum foil. Bake alongside the turkey for 30 minutes. Uncover and bake until the top is crisp, about 30 minutes longer.

To bake all the stuffing in a baking dish: Preheat an oven to 325°F (165°C). Butter a 13-by-9-by-2-inch (33-by-23-by-5-cm) baking dish and spoon the stuffing into it. Cover with foil and bake for 30 minutes. Uncover and bake until the top is crisp, about 30 minutes longer.

Makes about 12 cups (5 lb/2.5 kg) stuffing, enough for a 16 lb (8 kg) turkey; serves 8–10

Pear Upside-down Spice Cake

6 tablespoons (3 oz/90 g) plus ½ cup (4 oz/125 g) unsalted butter

1¼ cups (9 oz/275 g) firmly packed golden brown sugar

2 firm but ripe pears such as Anjou or Bartlett (Williams'), peeled, quartered, cored and thinly sliced

1½ cups (6 oz/185 g) cake (soft-wheat) flour

1⅛ teaspoons baking powder

¼ teaspoon baking soda (bicarbonate of soda)

4 teaspoons ground cinnamon

1 teaspoon ground ginger

½ teaspoon ground cloves

½ teaspoon salt

½ cup (4 fl oz/125 ml) milk

1 teaspoon vanilla extract (essence)

1 egg

½ cup (5½ oz/170 g) light molasses

1 tablespoon grated orange zest

¼ cup (1¼ oz/37 g) chopped crystallized ginger

whipped cream or vanilla ice cream

Preheat an oven to 350°F (180°C). Select a springform pan 10 inches (25 cm) in diameter and line with aluminum foil. Use one piece for the bottom and another for the sides, cutting the foil to fit and pressing it into the pan. Butter the foil.

In a small, heavy saucepan over low heat, melt the 6 tablespoons (3 oz/90 g) butter. Add ¾ cup (6 oz/185 g) of the brown sugar and stir until well blended. Pour into the foil-lined pan. Arrange the pear slices atop the syrup in the pan.

Sift together the flour, baking powder, baking soda, cinnamon, ground ginger, cloves and salt into a bowl. Combine the milk and vanilla in a small bowl. In a large bowl, using an electric mixer set on high speed, beat together the remaining ½ cup (4 oz/125 g) butter and ½ cup (3 oz/90 g) brown sugar until light and fluffy, about 3 minutes. Add the egg and beat until well blended. Add the molasses and orange zest and beat until fully combined. Mix in the dry ingredients in 2 batches alternately with the milk mixture, beginning and ending with the dry ingredients. Using a rubber spatula, fold in the crystallized ginger.

Pour the batter evenly over the pears in the pan, being careful not to disturb the pears.

Bake the cake until a toothpick inserted into the center comes out clean, about 55 minutes. Transfer to a wire rack to cool for 5 minutes. Run a small knife between the cake and the foil to loosen the cake. Turn out the cake onto the rack. Let cool for at least 30 minutes.

Serve the cake warm or at room temperature with whipped cream or ice cream.

Makes one 10-inch (25-cm) cake; serves 8–10

Corn Muffins with Dried Cranberries and Pecans

1 cup (5 oz/155 g) yellow cornmeal

1 cup (5 oz/155 g) unbleached all-purpose (plain) flour

⅓ cup (3 oz/90 g) sugar

2½ teaspoons baking powder

½ teaspoon salt

1 cup (8 fl oz/250 ml) buttermilk

6 tablespoons (3 oz/90 g) unsalted butter, melted

1 egg, lightly beaten

1 teaspoon grated orange zest

½ cup (2 oz/60 g) dried cranberries

½ cup (2 oz/60 g) chopped pecans

Orange zest and cranberries add a festive touch to muffins designed especially for the holiday bread basket. They can be made 1 day ahead and stored at room temperature. Be sure to cool them completely, then wrap tightly.

🍂

Preheat an oven to 425°F (220°C). Line 12 standard muffin cups with aluminum foil or paper liners.

Sift together the cornmeal, flour, sugar, baking powder and salt into a large bowl. Make a well in the center. Add the buttermilk, melted butter, egg and orange zest to the well. Using a wooden spoon, stir just until all the ingredients are combined. Mix in the dried cranberries and pecans.

Spoon the batter into the prepared cups, filling each about two-thirds full. Bake until golden brown and firm to the touch, about 20 minutes. Remove from the oven and let cool slightly in the pan on a wire rack. Serve warm or at room temperature.

Makes 12 muffins

Maple Spice Pecan Pie

The contrast of sweet maple syrup and tart lemon, plus a hint of nutmeg, transforms the standard pecan pie into something distinctive.

FOR THE PASTRY:

1½ cups (7½ oz/235 g) all-purpose (plain) flour

1 tablespoon sugar

½ teaspoon salt

¼ teaspoon ground nutmeg

1 tablespoon grated lemon zest

5 tablespoons (2½ oz/75 g) unsalted butter, chilled, cut into ½-inch (12-mm) pieces

3 tablespoons vegetable shortening, chilled, cut into ½-inch (12-mm) pieces

3 tablespoons ice water, or as needed

FOR THE FILLING:

3 eggs

¾ cup (6 oz/185 g) firmly packed dark brown sugar

1 cup (11 oz/345 g) pure maple syrup

3 tablespoons unsalted butter, melted

1 tablespoon fresh lemon juice

1 teaspoon vanilla extract (essence)

¾ teaspoon ground nutmeg

¼ teaspoon salt

1½ cups (6 oz/185 g) coarsely chopped pecans

To make the pastry, in a food processor fitted with the metal blade, combine the flour, sugar, salt, nutmeg and lemon zest. Process to mix. Add the butter and shortening and, using on-off pulses, cut them in until pea-sized pieces form. With the motor running, gradually add 3 tablespoons ice water and process just until the dough begins to hold together, adding more water by teaspoons, if needed. Form into a ball and flatten into a disk. Wrap in plastic wrap and refrigerate for at least 1 hour or for up to 1 day.

Place the dough disk between sheets of waxed paper and roll out into a round 12 inches (30 cm) in diameter. Peel off the top sheet of paper and, using the bottom sheet, transfer the round to a pie pan 9 inches (23 cm) in diameter. Peel off the paper and press the pastry gently onto the bottom and sides of the pan. Fold the edges under and crimp decoratively. Pierce the bottom and sides of the pastry in a few places with a fork. Freeze the crust for at least 30 minutes or cover and freeze for up to 3 days.

Preheat an oven to 450°F (230°C). Bake the crust until pale gold, about 15 minutes. Transfer to a wire rack to cool completely. Reduce the oven temperature to 350°F (180°C).

To make the filling, in a large bowl, whisk together the eggs and brown sugar until the sugar dissolves. Add the maple syrup, butter, lemon juice, vanilla, nutmeg and salt and whisk to blend. Mix in the pecans. Pour the filling into the crust. Bake until the filling is puffed and set, about 35 minutes. Transfer to the rack and let cool completely before serving.

Makes one 9-inch (23-cm) pie; serves 8–10

Baked Pears with Custard Sauce

FOR THE CUSTARD SAUCE:

2 cups (16 fl oz/500 ml) milk

6 egg yolks

½ cup (4 oz/125 g) sugar

1 tablespoon crème de cacao, Cointreau,
Grand Marnier or other liqueur

FOR THE PEARS:

2 cups (16 fl oz/500 ml) water

2 cups (1 lb/500 g) sugar

1 piece fresh ginger, about 3 inches
(7.5 cm) long, peeled and cut into 4
pieces

juice of 1 lemon

8–10 small or medium-sized firm but
ripe pears such as Comice, Bartlett
(Williams') or Bosc

small fresh mint sprigs

For this recipe from Chuck Williams, vanilla extract (essence) can be substituted for the liqueur in the custard sauce.

To make the custard sauce, in a heavy saucepan over medium heat, warm the milk just until bubbles appear along the edges of the pan. Remove from the heat. In a large bowl, combine the egg yolks and sugar and whisk until very light. Continuing to beat, gradually add the hot milk. Pour into the saucepan and place over medium-low heat. Cook, stirring constantly, just until the mixture thickens enough to coat the back of a spoon, about 5 minutes. Immediately remove from the heat and pour into a clean bowl; stir for a few seconds. Stir in the liqueur and cover with plastic wrap placed directly on the surface of the custard. Set aside to cool.

Preheat an oven to 350°F (180°C).

To prepare the pears, in a saucepan over medium heat, combine the water and sugar. Bring to a boil, stirring until the sugar dissolves. Add the ginger, reduce the heat to low and cook at a bare simmer, uncovered, until the ginger is translucent, 20–25 minutes. Remove from the heat.

Meanwhile, place the lemon juice in a large bowl. Peel the pears, cut in half lengthwise and remove the core and the stem and blossom ends. Place in the bowl and turn in the lemon juice to coat well. Arrange the pear halves in a large, shallow baking dish, core side up. Spoon the ginger syrup over the pears. Bake, basting every 5–6 minutes with the pan syrup, until tender, 20–25 minutes. Remove from the oven and let cool to room temperature.

To serve, divide the pear halves among dessert plates. Top with the custard sauce and garnish with mint sprigs.

Serves 8–10

Herbed Corn Bread

2 cups (10 oz/315 g) yellow cornmeal

1 cup (5 oz/155 g) all-purpose (plain) flour

⅓ cup (3 oz/90 g) sugar

1 tablespoon baking powder

¾ teaspoon salt

½ teaspoon baking soda (bicarbonate of soda)

1 teaspoon dried sage

1 teaspoon dried marjoram

1 teaspoon freshly ground pepper

½ cup (4 oz/125 g) butter, chilled, cut into ½-inch (12-mm) pieces

1½ cups (12 fl oz/375 ml) buttermilk

3 eggs

Delicious with dinner, this tender corn bread is also used for making the herbed corn bread and red pepper stuffing (recipe on page 58).

Preheat an oven to 400°F (200°C). Butter an 11-by-7-inch (28-by-18-cm) baking dish.

In a food processor fitted with the metal blade, combine the cornmeal, flour, sugar, baking powder, salt, baking soda, sage, marjoram and pepper. Process to mix. Add the butter and, using on-off pulses, cut in the butter until the mixture resembles coarse meal. In a large bowl, whisk together the buttermilk and eggs until blended. Add the cornmeal mixture and stir until thoroughly combined. Alternatively, to make by hand, in a large bowl, combine the cornmeal, flour, sugar, baking powder, salt, baking soda, sage, marjoram and pepper. Stir to blend. Add the butter and, using your fingertips, blend into the dry ingredients until the mixture resembles coarse meal. In a bowl, whisk together the buttermilk and eggs. Add to the cornmeal mixture and, using a wooden spoon, stir until thoroughly combined.

Transfer the batter to the prepared dish. Bake until golden brown on top and a toothpick inserted into the center comes out clean, about 30 minutes. Remove from the oven and let cool in the pan on a wire rack. Cut into squares and serve warm or at room temperature.

Serves 8–10

Apple-Cranberry Crisp

1¼ cups (4 oz/125 g) old-fashioned
  rolled oats
1 cup (7 oz/220 g) plus 2 tablespoons
  firmly packed dark brown sugar
¾ cup (4 oz/125 g) plus 1 tablespoon
  all-purpose (plain) flour
1¼ teaspoons ground cinnamon
1¼ teaspoons ground cardamom
¼ teaspoon salt
¾ cup (6 oz/185 g) unsalted butter,
  at room temperature
¾ cup (3 oz/90 g) sliced (flaked) almonds
4 lb (2 kg) tart apples such as pippin or
  Granny Smith, peeled, quartered,
  cored and sliced
1 bag (12 oz/375 g) cranberries (about
  3 cups)
⅔ cup (5 oz/155 g) granulated sugar
vanilla ice cream

*A deep-dish dessert of seasonal fruit baked with a crumbly
oat, almond, sugar and spice topping is as simple to make as
it is delicious.*

Preheat an oven to 375°F (190°C). Butter a 13-by-9-by-2-inch (33-by-23-by-5-cm) baking dish or a 3-qt (3-l) baking dish with sides 2 inches (5 mm) deep.

In a bowl, combine the oats, brown sugar, ¾ cup (4 oz/125 g) flour, ½ teaspoon of the cinnamon, ½ teaspoon of the cardamom and salt. Add the butter and, using your fingers, rub the ingredients together until the mixture is the consistency of coarse crumbs. Mix in the almonds.

In a large bowl, combine the apples, cranberries and granulated sugar and the remaining 1 tablespoon flour, remaining ¾ teaspoon cinnamon and remaining ¾ teaspoon cardamom. Stir to mix well. Transfer to the prepared dish. Spread the oat mixture evenly over the fruit.

Bake until the topping is golden brown and the apples are tender, about 55 minutes. Serve warm or at room temperature with scoops of vanilla ice cream.

Serves 8–10

(tastes like fruit cake) ★★

Orange, Walnut and Pear Pumpkin Bread

2 cups (14 oz/440 g) firmly packed golden brown sugar

1½ cups (12 oz/375 g) canned unsweetened solid-pack pumpkin purée

½ cup (4 fl oz/125 ml) vegetable oil

2 eggs

2 teaspoons baking soda (bicarbonate of soda)

1¼ teaspoons ground ginger

¾ teaspoon ground cardamom

4 teaspoons grated orange zest

½ teaspoon salt

1 cup (4 oz/125 g) walnuts, chopped

½ lb (250 g) dried pears, chopped (about 1½ cups)

2½ cups (12½ oz/390 g) all-purpose (plain) flour

orange zest strips, optional

The recipe makes 2 loaves; enjoy the second one for breakfast the next day. The loaves can also be wrapped tightly in aluminum foil and refrigerated for up to 3 days. Toasted, skinned and chopped hazelnuts (filberts) are a good substitute for the walnuts in this tender, slightly sweet bread.

Preheat an oven to 350°F (180°C). Butter and flour two 4½-by-8½-by-2½-inch (11.5-by-21.5-by-6-cm) loaf pans.

In a large bowl, using a wooden spoon, stir together the brown sugar, pumpkin purée, oil, eggs, baking soda, ginger, cardamom, grated orange zest and salt until well mixed. Add the walnuts and pears and stir to distribute evenly. Add the flour and stir just until blended; do not overmix. Divide the batter evenly between the prepared pans.

Bake until a toothpick inserted into the center comes out clean, about 55 minutes. Transfer to wire racks to cool for 10 minutes. Turn out the loaves onto the racks and let cool completely. Cut into slices, arrange on a serving platter and garnish with orange zest strips, if desired.

Makes 2 loaves

Ginger-Molasses Pumpkin Pie

FOR THE PASTRY:

1½ cups (7½ oz/235 g) all-purpose
(plain) flour

½ teaspoon salt

5 tablespoons (2½ oz/75 g) unsalted
butter, chilled

3 tablespoons vegetable shortening, chilled

3 tablespoons ice water, or as needed

FOR THE FILLING:

1 can (16 oz/500 g) unsweetened solid-
pack pumpkin purée

½ cup (3½ oz/105 g) plus 2 tablespoons
firmly packed golden brown sugar

1 tablespoon all-purpose (plain) flour

1 teaspoon ground ginger

½ teaspoon ground cinnamon

½ teaspoon ground nutmeg

½ teaspoon salt

3 eggs

1 cup (8 fl oz/250 ml) heavy (double)
cream

¼ cup (2 fl oz/60 ml) milk

¼ cup (3 oz/90 g) dark molasses

1½ teaspoons vanilla extract (essence)

FOR THE TOPPING:

1 cup (8 fl oz/250 ml) heavy (double)
cream, chilled

3 tablespoons firmly packed golden
brown sugar

1 tablespoon vanilla extract (essence)

½ cup (2½ oz/75 g) crystallized ginger

*T*o make the pastry, in a food processor fitted with the metal blade, mix the flour and salt. Cut the butter and shortening in ½-inch (12-mm) pieces. Add to the flour; process until pea-sized pieces form. With the motor running, gradually add 3 tablespoons ice water; process just until the dough begins to hold together, adding more water by teaspoons, if needed. Form into a ball and then flatten into a disk. Wrap in plastic wrap and refrigerate for at least 30 minutes or for up to 1 day.

Roll the dough between sheets of waxed paper into a round 13 inches (33 cm) in diameter. Transfer to a 10-inch (25-cm) pie pan and discard the paper. Press the pastry gently into the pan and fold the edges under. Crimp decoratively or brush with water and press on shapes cut from leftover dough. Pierce the pastry in a few places with a fork. Freeze the crust for at least 30 minutes or cover and freeze for up to 3 days.

Preheat an oven to 450°F (230°C). Bake the crust until pale golden, about 15 minutes. Transfer to a wire rack and let cool completely. Reduce the oven temperature to 375°F (190°C).

To make the filling, in a large bowl, mix the pumpkin purée, brown sugar, flour, ginger, cinnamon, nutmeg and salt until smooth. Whisk in the eggs, cream, milk, molasses and vanilla. Pour into the cooled crust. Bake for 20 minutes. Reduce the oven temperature to 325°F (165°C) and bake until the filling no longer jiggles in the center when the pan is shaken, about 30 minutes longer. Transfer to a wire rack and let cool.

To make the topping, in a large bowl, combine the cream, brown sugar and vanilla. Using a whisk or an electric mixer set on high speed, beat until soft peaks form. Mince the ginger and fold into the whipped cream. Cover and refrigerate if not using immediately.

Cut the pie into wedges and serve with the topping.

Makes one 10-inch (25-cm) pie; serves 8–10

Old-fashioned Gingerbread with Rum Whipped Cream

3 cups (15 oz/470 g) all-purpose (plain) flour

1½ teaspoons baking powder

4 teaspoons ground ginger

2 teaspoons ground cinnamon

½ teaspoon ground allspice

½ teaspoon ground cloves

¾ teaspoon baking soda (bicarbonate of soda)

¾ teaspoon salt

¾ cup (6 oz/185 g) unsalted butter, at room temperature

¾ cup (6 oz/185 g) firmly packed light brown sugar

2 eggs

1 cup (11 oz/345 g) plus 2 tablespoons dark molasses

4 teaspoons grated orange zest

1 cup (8 fl oz/250 ml) plus 2 tablespoons buttermilk

½ cup (2½ oz/75 g) chopped crystallized ginger

FOR THE WHIPPED CREAM:

1 cup (8 fl oz/250 ml) heavy (double) cream, chilled

3 tablespoons firmly packed light brown sugar

1 tablespoon dark rum

1 tablespoon vanilla extract (essence)

Dark molasses and crystallized ginger give this gingerbread a robust flavor. For extra color and texture, add 2 cups (8 oz/250 g) chopped fresh cranberries to the batter.

Preheat an oven to 350°F (180°C). Butter and flour a 13-by-9-by-2-inch (33-by-23-by-5-cm) baking dish.

Sift together the flour, baking powder, ground ginger, cinnamon, allspice, cloves, baking soda and salt into a bowl. In a large bowl, using an electric mixer set on high speed, beat the butter until light and fluffy, about 2 minutes. Add the brown sugar and beat until fluffy, about 2 minutes longer. Beat in the eggs one at a time, then beat in the molasses and orange zest until well combined. Mix in the dry ingredients in 3 batches alternately with the buttermilk, beginning and ending with the dry ingredients. Using a rubber spatula, fold in the crystallized ginger.

Pour the batter into the prepared dish, spreading it evenly and smoothing the surface. Bake until springy to the touch, about 50 minutes. Transfer to a wire rack to cool.

To prepare the whipped cream, in a large bowl, combine the cream and brown sugar. Using an electric mixer set on high speed, beat until stiff peaks form. Add the rum and vanilla and beat again until stiff peaks form.

Cut the gingerbread into squares and serve warm or at room temperature with the whipped cream.

Serves 12

Chive Cream Biscuits

2 cups (10 oz/315 g) all-purpose (plain)
  flour, plus flour for kneading
¼ cup (⅓ oz/10 g) minced fresh chives
  or ¼ cup (¾ oz/20 g) green (spring)
  onions, including tender green tops
1 tablespoon baking powder
½ teaspoon salt
1 teaspoon freshly ground pepper, plus
  pepper to taste
about 1⅓ cups (11 fl oz/330 ml) heavy
  (double) cream
2 tablespoons butter, melted

For an extra burst of chive flavor, mix minced chives into butter for spreading on these light biscuits.

*P*osition a rack in the upper third of an oven and preheat to 425°F (220°C).

In a large bowl, combine the 2 cups (10 oz/315 g) flour, chives or green onions, baking powder, salt and 1 teaspoon pepper. Using a wooden spoon, mix well. Gradually stir in enough cream to form a dough that comes together into a ball.

Transfer the dough to a floured work surface. Knead gently until smooth, about 10 turns. Roll out the dough ½ inch (12 mm) thick. Using a round or heart-shaped biscuit cutter 2½ inches (6 cm) in diameter, cut out biscuits. Transfer the biscuits to an ungreased baking sheet, spacing them 1 inch (2.5 cm) apart. Gather together the scraps and roll out ½ inch (12 mm) thick. Cut out additional biscuits and transfer them to the baking sheet as well.

Brush the biscuits with the melted butter and sprinkle with pepper to taste. Bake until light brown, about 15 minutes. Remove from the oven and serve hot or transfer to a wire rack to cool and serve warm.

Makes about 12 biscuits

Apple Pie with Lemon and Vanilla

FOR THE PASTRY:

2⅔ cups (13½ oz/420 g) all-purpose (plain) flour

2 tablespoons sugar

½ teaspoon salt

½ cup (4 oz/125 g) vegetable shortening, chilled, cut into pieces

½ cup (4 oz/125 g) unsalted butter, chilled, cut into pieces

1 egg

3 tablespoons ice water, or as needed

FOR THE FILLING:

1½ lb (750 g) tart apples, peeled, quartered, cored and cut into slices ¼ inch (6 mm) thick

1½ lb (750 g) sweet, juicy apples, peeled, quartered, cored and cut into slices ¼ inch (6 mm) thick

¾ cup (6 oz/185 g) sugar

¼ cup (1½ oz/45 g) all-purpose (plain) flour

1 teaspoon grated lemon zest

1 tablespoon fresh lemon juice

½ teaspoon ground cinnamon

½ teaspoon ground nutmeg

1 vanilla bean, halved lengthwise

FOR GLAZING THE PASTRY:

1 tablespoon sugar

¼ teaspoon ground cinnamon

¼ teaspoon ground nutmeg

1 tablespoon milk

*T*o make the pastry, in a food processor fitted with the metal blade, combine the flour, sugar and salt. Process to mix. Add the shortening and butter and, using on-off pulses, cut them in until the mixture resembles coarse meal. In a small bowl, whisk together the egg and 3 tablespoons ice water until blended. With the motor running, gradually pour into the flour mixture and process until moist clumps form. Add more water by tea-spoons if the dough is too dry. Form into a ball and divide in half. Flatten each half into a disk. Wrap separately in plastic wrap and refrigerate for at least 1 hour or for up to 1 day.

Position a rack in the bottom third of an oven and preheat to 400°F (200°C). To make the filling, in a large bowl, combine the apples, sugar, flour, lemon zest and juice, cinnamon and nutmeg. Scrape the vanilla bean seeds into the bowl. Mix well.

Roll 1 dough disk between sheets of waxed paper into a round 13 inches (33 cm) in diameter. Transfer the pastry to a deep-dish pie plate 9 inches (23 cm) in diameter and 2 inches (5 cm) deep, discarding the paper, and gently press into the pan. Trim the overhang to ½ inch (12 mm). Brush the edges lightly with water. Transfer the filling to the plate, mounding it slightly in the center. Similarly roll out the second dough disk 12 inches (30 cm) in diameter. Place atop the apples and trim the overhang to 1 inch (2.5 cm). Fold the top crust edge under the bottom crust edge; press and crimp decoratively. Cut several slits in the top crust. Place the pie on a baking sheet. Bake for 45 minutes.

To make the glaze, in a small bowl, stir together the sugar, cinnamon and nutmeg. Brush the top crust with the milk, then sprinkle with the sugar mixture. Bake until the crust is golden brown, about 20 minutes longer; cover the edges with foil if browning too quickly. Cool on a wire rack, then serve.

Makes one 9-inch (23-cm) deep-dish pie; serves 8

Lemon and Molasses Whole-Wheat Biscuits

2 cups (10 oz/315 g) all-purpose (plain) flour, plus flour for kneading

1 cup (5 oz/155 g) whole-wheat (wholemeal) flour

⅓ cup (2½ oz/75 g) firmly packed dark brown sugar

1 tablespoon plus ¾ teaspoon baking powder

¾ teaspoon baking soda (bicarbonate of soda)

½ teaspoon salt

1 tablespoon grated lemon zest

¾ cup (4 oz/125 g) dried pitted sour cherries or dried currants

6 tablespoons (3 oz/90 g) unsalted butter

3 tablespoons dark molasses

1 cup (8 fl oz/250 ml) plus 2 tablespoons buttermilk

1 egg beaten with 1 tablespoon buttermilk for glaze

Dried sour cherries transform these wonderful homespun biscuits into something memorable for the holiday meal.

⌐

Preheat an oven to 425°F (220°C).

In a large bowl, combine the 2 cups (10 oz/315 g) all-purpose flour, whole-wheat flour, brown sugar, baking powder, baking soda, salt, lemon zest and cherries or currants. Using a wooden spoon, mix well. In a small saucepan, combine the butter and molasses. Place over low heat until the butter melts.

Meanwhile, pour the buttermilk into a measuring pitcher. Add the melted butter mixture and stir to mix. Gradually add the buttermilk mixture to the flour mixture, stirring just until blended and the dough comes together in a ball.

Transfer the dough to a generously floured work surface. Knead gently until smooth, about 20 turns. Roll out the dough to a generous ½ inch (12 mm) thick. Using a round biscuit cutter 2½ inches (6 cm) in diameter, cut out biscuits. Transfer the biscuits to an ungreased baking sheet, spacing them 1 inch (2.5 cm) apart. Gather together the scraps and roll out to a generous ½ inch (12 mm) thick. Cut out additional biscuits and transfer to the baking sheet as well.

Brush the biscuits with the egg glaze. Bake until just firm to the touch, about 20 minutes. Remove from the oven and serve hot or transfer to a wire rack to cool and serve warm.

Makes about 16 biscuits

Cashew, Almond and Walnut Caramel Tart

FOR THE PASTRY:

1¼ cups (6½ oz/200 g) unbleached
    all-purpose (plain) flour

3 tablespoons sugar

2 teaspoons grated lemon zest

½ cup (4 oz/125 g) unsalted butter,
    chilled, cut into ½-inch (12-mm)
    pieces

2 egg yolks

2 teaspoons ice water

FOR THE FILLING:

½ cup (4 oz/125 g) unsalted butter

½ cup (3½ oz/105 g) plus 2 tablespoons
    firmly packed dark brown sugar

¼ cup (3 oz/90 g) honey

1 cup (5½ oz/170 g) blanched whole
    almonds, toasted (*see glossary, page 106*)

1 cup (4 oz/125 g) walnuts, toasted
    (*see glossary, page 106*)

¾ cup (4 oz/125 g) salted roasted
    cashews

2 tablespoons heavy (double) cream

*T*o make the pastry, in a food processor fitted with the metal blade, combine the flour, sugar and lemon zest. Process to mix. Add the butter and, using on-off pulses, cut in the butter until the mixture resembles coarse meal. In a small bowl, whisk together the yolks and ice water until blended. Gradually pour into the flour mixture and process just until the dough begins to gather together. Form the dough into a ball and flatten into a disk. Wrap in plastic wrap and refrigerate for at least 30 minutes or for up to 1 day.

Butter a tart pan 11 inches (28 cm) in diameter with a removable bottom. Roll the dough disk between sheets of waxed paper into a round ⅛ inch (3 mm) thick. Peel off the top sheet and transfer the round to the prepared pan. Peel off the paper and press the pastry gently into the pan. Trim the edges even with the rim. Pierce the crust in a few places with a fork. Freeze for at least 30 minutes or cover and freeze for up to 3 days.

Preheat an oven to 400°F (200°C). Bake the crust until golden brown, about 18 minutes. Transfer to a wire rack to cool completely, then place on a baking sheet. Reduce the oven temperature to 350°F (180°C).

To make the filling, in a saucepan over low heat, combine the butter, brown sugar and honey; stir until the sugar dissolves. Raise the heat to high and whisk until the mixture comes to a boil. Boil without stirring until large bubbles form, about 1 minute. Remove from the heat. Stir in the almonds, walnuts, cashews and cream. Immediately pour into the crust.

Bake until the filling bubbles, about 20 minutes. Transfer to the rack to cool for about 30 minutes. Remove the pan sides and cool the tart completely. Transfer to a plate and serve.

Makes one 11-inch (28-cm) tart; serves 8–10

Glossary

The following glossary defines terms specifically as they relate to Thanksgiving recipes, with a special emphasis on major and unusual ingredients.

APPLES

A range of autumn and winter apples graces the Thanksgiving table. Among the most widely available are the following varieties used in this book:

Fuji Mostly red apple with yellow highlights and a crisp, juicy, sweet flesh; eaten raw or used in cooking.

Gala Sweet, juicy apple with red-blushed yellow skin; used in salads and pies.

Golden Delicious Pale yellow-green apple with a crisp, light, juicy texture; eaten raw or used in baked desserts.

Granny Smith Bright green apple with juicy, tart, very crisp flesh; eaten raw or used in salads, stuffings or baked desserts.

Pippin Green to yellow-green apple with a slightly tart taste; used in salads, stuffings and baked desserts.

BELL PEPPERS

Sweet-fleshed, bell-shaped member of the pepper family. Also known as capsicum. Most common in the unripe green form, although ripened red and yellow varieties are also available. Creamy pale yellow, orange and purple-black types may also be found.

To prepare a raw bell pepper, cut in half lengthwise with a sharp knife. Pull out the stem section from each half, along with the cluster of seeds attached to it. Remove any remaining seeds and any thin white membranes, or ribs, to which they are attached. Cut the pepper halves into quarters, strips or thin slices, as called for in the specific recipe.

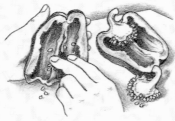

BUTTER, UNSALTED

For the bread and dessert recipes in this book, unsalted, or sweet, butter is preferred.

BUTTERMILK

Form of cultured low-fat or nonfat milk that contributes a tangy flavor and thick, creamy texture to batters and doughs. Its acidity also provides a boost to leavening agents, adding extra lightness.

CHESTNUTS

Whole peeled chestnuts or chestnut pieces are available in cans and jars in specialty-food shops and the specialty-food sections of markets. Fresh chestnuts are sold in the produce sections of markets. Their glossy brown shells must be removed before use.

To peel chestnuts, use a sharp knife to score an X in the shell on the flat side of each chestnut, then bake or boil.

To bake the chestnuts, place in a baking pan large enough to hold them in a single layer, add ½ cup (4 fl oz/125 ml) water and bake in a preheated 400°F (200°C) oven until the shells begin to turn brittle and peel back at the X, about 20 minutes. While the nuts are still warm, peel off the brittle shells and the furry skin directly beneath them. Do not allow the chestnuts to cool or they will be difficult to peel.

To boil the chestnuts, cook in boiling water to cover for about 15 minutes. Turn off the heat but leave the chestnuts in the water to keep warm and facilitate peeling. One at a time, peel the chestnuts.

DRIED FRUITS

Intensely flavored and satisfyingly chewy, many forms of sun-dried or kiln-dried fruits may be added to enhance the taste or texture of savory and sweet Thanksgiving dishes. Select recently dried and packaged fruits, which have a softer texture than older dried fruits. Usually found in specialty-food shops or baking sections of food stores. Some of the most popular options include:

Cherries, Sour Ripe, tart red cherries that have been pitted and dried—usually in a kiln, with a little sugar added to help preserve them—to a consistency and shape like those of raisins.

Cranberries Resembling raisins in shape, these tart, chewy berries are popular additions to baked goods, sauces and chutneys.

Currants Produced from a variety of small, seedless grapes, these dried fruits are reminiscent of tiny raisins, but with a stronger, tarter flavor. If currants are unavailable, substitute raisins.

Dates Sweet, deep brown fruits of the date palm tree, with a naturally thick, sticky consistency that recalls candied fruit. Sometimes available pitted and chopped.

Figs Compact form of the succulent black or golden summertime fruits, distinguished by a slightly crunchy texture derived from their tiny seeds.

Pears Halved, seeded and flattened fruits that retain the distinctive profile of their fresh counterpart.

Prunes Variety of dried plum, with a rich, dark, moist flesh.

Raisins, Golden Variety of dried grapes, popular as a snack on their own and in baked goods. Also called sultanas.

CRANBERRIES
Round, deep red, tart berries, grown primarily in wet, sandy coastal lands—or bogs—in the northeastern United States. Available fresh during the late autumn and frozen year-round.

GREEN BEANS
Fresh beans, also known as string beans or snap beans, are harvested when their pods and the seeds inside are immature, still tender and edible. The Blue Lake variety is particularly prized for its bright color, fresh sweet flavor and crisp texture.

HERBS
A wide variety of fresh and dried herbs adds character to Thanksgiving dishes.

Bay Leaves Dried whole leaves of the bay laurel tree. Pungent and spicy, they flavor simmered dishes, including stock. The French variety, available in specialty-food shops, has a milder, sweeter flavor than California bay leaves. Discard the leaves before serving.

Marjoram Pungent, aromatic herb used dried or fresh to season poultry, savory baked goods and such Thanksgiving side dishes as stuffings and vegetables.

Parsley This popular fresh herb is found in two varieties, the readily available curly-leaf type and a flat-leaf type. The latter, also known as Italian parsley, has a more pronounced flavor and is preferred.

Rosemary Mediterranean herb, used fresh or dried, with an aromatic flavor well suited to vegetables and roast turkey and other poultry.

Sage Pungent herb, used fresh or dried, that goes particularly well with poultry and vegetables.

Tarragon Fragrant, distinctively sweet herb used fresh or dried as a seasoning for salads, seafood, dressings and vegetables.

Thyme Fragrant, clean-tasting, small-leaved herb popular as a seasoning for salads, poultry, ham and vegetables; it is used fresh or dried.

To chop fresh herbs, first wash under cold running water and thoroughly shake dry. If the herb has leaves attached along woody stems, pull the leaves from the stems; otherwise, hold the stems together and gather the leaves into a compact bunch. Using a chef's knife, carefully cut across the bunch to chop the leaves coarsely. Discard the stems. For more finely chopped herbs, gather the coarsely chopped leaves together. Steadying the top of the knife blade with one hand, chop the herbs, rocking the blade and moving it back and forth in an arc until the desired fineness is reached.

To use dried herbs, crush them first in the palm of the hand to release their flavor. Or warm them in a frying pan and crush in a mortar with a pestle.

HONEY
The natural, sweet, syruplike substance produced by bees from flower nectar, honey subtly reflects the color, taste and aroma of the blossoms from which it was made. Milder varieties, such as clover and orange blossom,

are lighter in color and better suited to general cooking. Those derived from herb blossoms, such as thyme, have a more distinctively aromatic taste.

LEEKS
Sweet, moderately flavored member of the onion family, long and cylindrical with a pale white root end and dark green leaves. Select firm, unblemished leeks, small to medium in size. Grown in sandy soil, the leafy-topped, multilayered vegetables require thorough cleaning.

To trim and clean leeks, cut off the tough ends of the dark green leaves and the roots. Trim off the dark green leaves where they meet the slender pale green part of the stem. Starting about 1 inch (2.5 cm) from the root end, slit the leek lengthwise.

Vigorously swish the leek in a basin or sink filled with cold water. Drain and rinse again; check to make sure that no dirt remains within the tightly packed pale portion of the leaves.

MAPLE SYRUP
Syrup made from boiling the sap of the maple tree, with an inimitably rich flavor and intense sweetness. Buy maple syrup that is labeled "pure," rather than a blend.

MOLASSES
Thick, robust-tasting, syrupy sugarcane by-product of sugar refining. Light (unsulfured)

MUSHROOMS
With their meaty textures and rich, earthy flavors, mushrooms are used to enrich a variety of Thanksgiving dishes.

Chanterelle Subtly flavored, usually pale yellow, trumpet-shaped wild mushrooms 2–3 inches (5–7.5 cm) in length; also cultivated commercially.

Cultivated White Widely available in food markets and greengrocers; in their smallest form, with their caps still closed, these mushrooms are often descriptively called button mushrooms.

Oyster White, gray or pinkish mushrooms (1) with lily-shaped caps; sold fresh in Asian markets and well-stocked food stores. They have a tender texture and mild flavor faintly reminiscent of oysters.

(1)   (2)

Shiitake Meaty-flavored Asian mushrooms (2) with flat, dark brown caps usually 2–3 inches (5–7.5 cm) in diameter; available fresh with increasing frequency, particularly in Asian food shops. They are also sold dried, requiring soaking in warm water to cover for approximately 20 minutes before use.

molasses results from the first boiling of the syrup, dark molasses from the second boiling.

MUSTARD, DIJON
True Dijon mustard is made in Dijon, France, from dark brown mustard seeds (unless marked *blanc*) and white wine or wine vinegar. Fairly hot and sharp tasting, Dijon mustard and non-French blends labeled Dijon style are widely available in food stores.

NUTS
Rich and mellow in flavor, crisp and crunchy in texture, a wide variety of nuts complements Thanksgiving recipes.

Almonds Mellow, sweet nuts that are an important crop in California and are popular throughout the world. Sold whole (with their skins intact), and blanched (with their skins removed) and thinly sliced (flaked).

Cashews Kidney-shaped, crisp nuts with a slightly sweet and buttery flavor. Native to tropical America but grown throughout the world, primarily in India.

Hazelnuts Small, usually spherical nuts with a slightly sweet flavor. Grown in Italy, Spain and the United States. Also known as filberts.

Pecans Brown-skinned nuts with a distinctive sweet, rich flavor, crisp, slightly crumbly texture and crinkly surface. Native to the southern United States.

Pine Nuts Small, ivory seeds extracted from the cones of a species of pine tree, with a rich, slightly resinous flavor.

Walnuts Rich, crisp nuts with distinctively crinkled surfaces. English walnuts, the most familiar variety, are grown worldwide; the largest crops are in California.

To toast nuts, which brings out their full flavor and aroma, preheat an oven to 325°F (165°C). Spread the nuts in a single layer on a baking sheet and toast in the oven until they just begin to change color and are fragrant, 5–10 minutes. Remove from the oven and let cool to room temperature. Toasting such nuts as hazelnuts and walnuts also loosens the skins, which may be removed by wrapping the still-warm nuts in a kitchen towel and rubbing against them with the palms of your hands.

ONIONS
A range of onions add their mild and sweet or strong and pungent flavors to salads, soups, stuffings and other Thanksgiving dishes.

Green Also called spring onion or scallion, this variety (1) is harvested immature, leaves and all, before the bulbs have formed. Both green and white parts may be enjoyed raw or cooked for their mild but still pronounced onion flavor.

Red This mild, sweet onion (2) has purplish red skin and red-tinged white flesh. Also known as Spanish onion.

White Boiling This small onion (3), usually about 1 inch (2.5 cm) in diameter, has white skin and pungent white flesh.

Yellow Distinguished by its dry, yellowish brown skin, this popular onion (4) has strong-flavored white flesh.

(2)   (4)

(3)   (1)

PEARS
The subtle sweetness and texture of pears make them a particular treat of the Thanksgiving table.

Anjou Available from autumn through midspring, these are rich in flavor, with a hint of spice and a smooth texture; among the largest and plumpest of pears, they have short necks and thin, yellow-green skins.

Bartlett Also called Williams' pears, these medium-sized fruits (1) are shaped roughly like bells, with creamy yellow skins sometimes tinged in red; fine-textured, juicy and mild tasting, they are available in summer and autumn.

(2)   (1)

Bosc Long, slender, tapered variety (below) with yellow-and-russet skin and slightly grainy, solid-textured white flesh with a hint of acidity. A good cooking pear, the Bosc is sold from October through the winter.

Comice Available from autumn through early winter, these large, round, short-necked fruits (2) are sweet and juicy, and have greenish yellow skins tinged with red.

PARSNIPS
Root vegetable similar in shape and texture to the carrot, but with ivory flesh and an appealingly sweet flavor.

PUMPKIN PURÉE
Orange purée of pumpkin meat often used in pies, breads and other bakery items. Available canned in most food stores. For the recipes in this book, be sure to buy the unsweetened solid-pack variety.

RUTABAGAS
Root vegetable resembling a large **turnip,** with sweet, pale yellow flesh. Also known as swede or Swedish turnip.

SHALLOTS
Small member of the onion family with brownish skin, white flesh tinged with purple and a flavor resembling a cross between sweet onion and garlic.

SHERRY, DRY
A fortified, cask-aged wine, dry sherry is used as a flavoring in both savory dishes and desserts and is enjoyed as an aperitif.

SHORTENING, VEGETABLE
Solid vegetable fat sometimes used in place of or in combination with butter in batters and pastry doughs. The fat is said to "shorten" the flour, that is, to make it flaky and tender.

SQUASHES, WINTER
Native to the Americas, squashes are divided into two main types: thin-skinned summer squashes,

uch as zucchini (courgette) and attypan, and hard, tough-kinned winter squashes, which eature prominently on Thanks-giving tables. Among winter quashes, two of the most com-mon types, used in this book, are the acorn squash, a dark green, orange-fleshed variety shaped like a large acorn, approximately 6 inches (15 cm) in length, and the butternut (at right), a pale yellowish tan variety with yellow to orange flesh. Commonly

8–12 inches (20–30 cm) long, it has a broad bulblike base and a more slender neck.

deep orange flesh, resembling but not related to the true yams native to the Caribbean.

SPICES

Many different spices add enticing flavor to both savory and sweet dishes served at Thanksgiving.

Allspice Sweet spice of Carib-bean origin with a flavor sug-gesting a blend of cinnamon, cloves and nutmeg, hence its name. Available as whole dried berries or ground. When whole berries are used, they may be bruised—gently crushed with the bottom of a pan or other heavy instrument—to release more of their flavor.

Cardamom Sweet, exotic-tasting spice mainly used in Middle Eastern and Indian cooking and in Scandinavian baking. Its small, round seeds, which come enclosed inside a husklike pod, are best pur-chased whole, then ground with a spice grinder or in a mortar with a pestle as needed.

Cinnamon Popular sweet spice commonly used for flavoring baked goods. The aromatic bark of a type of evergreen tree, it is sold as whole dried strips—cinnamon sticks—or ground.

Cloves Rich and aromatic East African spice used whole or in its ground form to flavor sweet and savory recipes.

Cumin Middle Eastern spice with a strong, dusky, aromatic flavor. Sold ground or as small, crescent-shaped seeds.

Ginger The rhizome of the tropical ginger plant, which yields a sweet, strong-flavored spice. Ground, dried ginger is available in the spice section of most food stores. Candied or crystallized ginger is made by first preserving pieces of ginger in sugar syrup and then coating them with granulated sugar; it is available in specialty-food shops or in the baking or Asian food sections of well-stocked stores.

Nutmeg Popular baking spice that is the hard pit of the fruit of the nutmeg tree. May be bought already ground or, for fresher flavor, whole and then ground as needed.

Turmeric Pungent, earthy-flavored ground spice that, like saffron, adds a vibrant yellow color to any dish.

STOCK
Flavorful liquid derived from slowly simmering chicken, meat, fish or vegetables in water, along with herbs and aromatic ingre-dients such as **onions.** Used as the primary cooking liquid or moistening and flavoring agent in many recipes. Stock may be made fairly easily at home, to be frozen for future use. Good-quality canned stocks or broths, in regular or concentrated form, are also available; many tend to be saltier than homemade stock, so seek out those labeled "low-sodium" and, in recipes in which they are used, taste carefully for seasoning. Excellent stocks may also be found in the freezer section of better food stores.

SUGAR, BROWN
A rich-tasting granulated sugar combined with molasses in varying quantities to yield golden, light or dark brown sugar, with crystals varying from coarse to finely granulated.

SWEET POTATOES
Not true potatoes, although resembling them in form, these tuberous vegetables have light to deep red skin and pale yellow to orange flesh prized for its sweetness when cooked. The light-skinned variety is the most common. Yam-type sweet potatoes refer to those with dark skins and

TURNIPS
Creamy white root vegetable, tinged purple or green at its crown, with firm, pungent yet slightly sweet flesh. Generally cooked by boiling, braising or stewing. Choose smaller turnips that feel heavy for their size and are firm to the touch.

VANILLA
Vanilla beans are the dried aromatic pods of a variety of orchid. One of the most popular flavorings in dessert making, vanilla is commonly used in the form of an alcohol-based extract (essence). Be sure to purchase products labeled "pure vanilla extract." Vanilla extract or beans from Madagascar are the best.

ZEST
Thin, brightly colored, outermost layer of a citrus fruit's peel, containing most of its aromatic essential oils—a lively source of flavor. Zest may be removed with a simple tool known as a zester, drawn across the fruit's skin to remove the zest in thin strips;

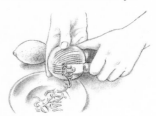

with a fine handheld grater; or in wide strips with a vegetable peeler or a paring knife held almost parallel to the fruit's skin. Zest removed with the latter two tools may then be thinly sliced or chopped on a cutting board.

Index

ACKNOWLEDGMENTS

The publishers would like to thank the following people for their generous assistance and support in producing this book: William Garry, Santiago Homsi Jr., Lorraine and Jud Puckett, Patty Draper, Patty Hill, Ken DellaPenta, Tina Schmitz, and the buyers and store managers for Pottery Barn and Williams-Sonoma stores.

The following kindly lent props for the photography: Biordi Art Imports, Candelier, Sue Fisher King, Chuck Williams, Williams-Sonoma and Pottery Barn.

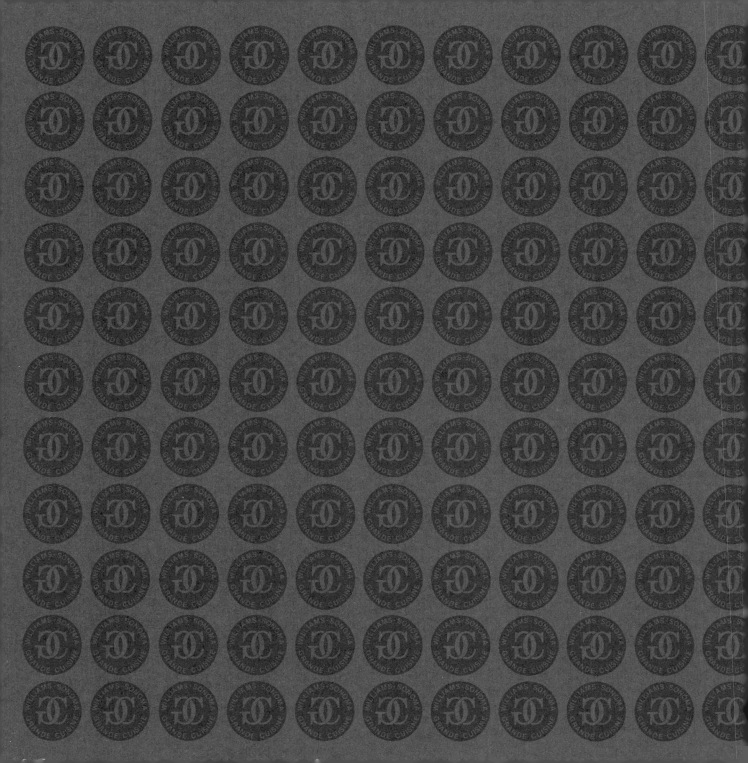